AMERICAN ESSAYS IN LITURGY

A Lyrical Vision

AMERICAN ESSAYS IN LITURGY

Series Editor, Edward Foley

A Lyrical Vision

The Music Documents of the US Bishops

Edward Foley, Capuchin

LITURGICAL PRESS
Collegeville, Minnesota

www.litpress.org

Cover design by Ann Blattner.

Excerpts from documents of the Second Vatican Council are from *Vatican Council II: The Basic Sixteen Documents*, by Austin Flannery, OP © 1996 (Costello Publishing Company, Inc.). Used with permission.

1	2	3	4	5	6	7	8	9

Library of Congress Cataloging-in-Publication Data

Foley, Edward.
    A lyrical vision : the music documents of the US Bishops / Edward Foley.
      p. cm. — (American essays in liturgy)
    ISBN 978-0-8146-3279-6 (pbk.)
    1. Church music—Catholic Church.   2. Church music—United States.
    I. Title.

ML3011.F65 2009
787.71'200973—dc22   2009010213

Contents

Introduction

The original intent of this project was to offer some commentary on the most recent music document of the US Bishops, *Sing to the Lord* (2007). As I began that work, tracing the influences and genealogy of the document, it became clear to me that it was inappropriate to consider this single work in isolation from its three predecessors—also from the US bishops—that were so foundational to it. Furthermore, the process of excavating *Sing to the Lord* not only provided the opportunity to tell something of the history of each of its forerunners but also allowed me to provide some narrative about individuals, groups, issues, and controversies that surrounded their composition and dissemination.

This process has allowed me to be in dialogue with many pioneers who shared various parts of this story. I am very grateful to those many individuals who were willing to be interviewed for this project, including Fr. William Bauman; Fr. Patrick Collins; Msgr. Donald Hansen; Fr. Lawrence Heiman, CPpS; Fr. Ron Krisman; Fr. Giles Pater; Fr. Frank Quinn, OP, (d. 2008); and Most Rev. Rembert Weakland, OSB. Besides the invaluable information I received from them, I also received gracious assistance from Ms. Mary Beth Kunde Anderson; Mr. Neil Borgstrom; Ms. Monique Brulin; Fr. James Chepponis; Fr. Michael Driscoll; Fr. Tom Elich; Prof. O. Fußangel; Fr. John Gurrieri; Mr. Alan Hommerding; Ms. Melody McMahon; Mr. Randall Mullin; Fr. Gilbert Ostdiek, OFM; Fr. Keith Pecklers, SJ; Msgr. Anthony Schermann; Fr. Jeoffrey Steel; Dr. Gordon Truitt; and Mr. Edmund Yates.

Sing to the Lord is the most recent in a series of remarkable documents from the US bishops on music and liturgy. Together with its three predecessor documents, *The Place of Music in Eucharistic Celebrations*,

Music in Catholic Worship, and *Liturgical Music Today*, it offers more than pastoral directives and musical insights into the corporate worship of Roman Catholics in this country. These documents collectively provide a lyrical vision for what musical liturgy can be in the unfolding reforms after the Second Vatican Council. May this vision well sustain us as together we ever sing to the Lord a new song.

Edward Foley, Capuchin
17 December 2008
The onset of the O Antiphons

1   The Forgotten Breakthrough

While *Music in Catholic Worship* (MCW) and subsequent documents from the United States bishops on music and liturgy are well celebrated and quite accessible to today's pastoral liturgists and musicians, the statement that began it all is largely fogotten and unknown. *The Place of Music in Eucharistic Celebrations* (PMEC) was published in 1968 by the US Bishops' Committee on the Liturgy and became foundational for the three documents that were to follow: MCW in 1972, *Liturgical Music Today* (LMT) in 1982, and *Sing to the Lord* (STTL) in 2007.

In this chapter we will examine the background of this foundational document before turning to a discussion of the structure and content of PMEC. We will also offer an initial evaluation of how PMEC has influenced developments within musical liturgy in the United States in succeeding decades. However, a complete appreciation of the import of this document is not possible until we have more thoroughly examined MCW and STTL. Only then can one begin to comprehend how foundational and influential PMEC has been, not only for the shaping of other documents from the Bishops' Committee on the Liturgy but also for influencing the way Roman Catholics in the United States think about, plan, and evaluate music in the liturgy.

The Background

Musicam Sacram

As we look back from the perspective of the early twenty-first century we can see that the developments in liturgy and music precipitated by the Second Vatican Council unfolded not only with amazing speed but also with quite unexpected breadth. Almost fifteen months to the day after Vatican II had issued the Constitution on the Sacred Liturgy (CSL) on 4 December 1963, the Sacred Congregation for Rites promulgated *Musicam Sacram* ("Sacred Music") on 5 March 1967.[1] This was the first and only instruction completely devoted to music issued by a Vatican Congregation in the wake of Vatican II. It both signaled the onset of significant changes within Roman Catholic musical liturgy and at the same time embodied theological and pastoral tensions, many of which continue to confront us.

Today *Musicam Sacram* might strike some as a tame, even backward-looking document. We must recognize, however, that *Musicam Sacram* was issued two years before the new Order of Mass was to appear in 1969. Thus it has to be understood primarily as a commentary on the Latin or Tridentine Mass that was universally celebrated by Catholics around the world at that time.[2] While a 1964 Vatican document had already made some modifications to that rite—for example, instructing clergy to omit Psalm 42 in the prayers at the foot of the altar, allowing the insertion of the prayer of the faithful if the local bishop allowed, and even authorizing the use of the vernacular at designated moments in the rite[3]—it was still the Tridentine Rite that was in force in 1965 and was the unquestionable context for *Musicam Sacram*'s instructions and directives. As that document itself notes, its instructions are to be observed "until reform of the entire *Ordo Missae* ["Order of Mass"]" takes place (IO, no. 48).

Despite its "interim" status and the fact that in some ways *Musicam Sacram* was looking back on a rite that was soon to be eclipsed by the new Order of Mass, it nonetheless sounded significant themes and directions that are still important for musical liturgy today. Notable, for example, is its eloquent commentary on music's effect within worship:

> A liturgical services takes on a nobler aspect when the rites are celebrated with singing, the ministers of each rank take their parts in them, and the congregation actively participates. This form of celebration

---

1. An English translation of this document is available in *Documents on the Liturgy 1963–1979: Conciliar, Papal, and Curial Texts* [hereafter DOL] (Collegeville: Liturgical Press, 1982), no. 508 (pp. 1293–1306).

2. For a further discussion of the historical and liturgical context of this document see my "*Musicam Sacram* Revisited: Anchor to the Past or Path to the Future," *Studia Canonica* 42, no. 1 (2008): 59–80.

3. *Inter Oecumenici* in DOL, no. 23 (pp. 88–110).

gives a more graceful expression to prayer . . . . It achieves a closer union of hearts through the union of voices. It raises the mind more readily to heavenly realities through the splendor of the rites. It makes the whole celebration a more striking symbol of the celebration to come in the heavenly Jerusalem. (MS, no. 5)

Another important statement is its classic exposition of what constitutes "solemnity" in worship:

The real solemnity of a liturgical service, it should be kept in mind, depends not on a more ornate musical style or more ceremonial splendor but on a worthy and reverent celebration. This means respect for the integrity of the rites, that is, carrying out each of the parts in keeping with its proper character. (MS, no. 11)

Then there are the many passages in *Musicam Sacram* affirming that linchpin of the conciliar reform, the active participation of the people. One of these is found in paragraph 15:

The faithful carry out their proper liturgical function by offering their complete, conscious, and active participation. The very nature of the liturgy demands this and it is the right and duty of Christian people by reason of their baptism. This participation must be:

a. internal, that is, the faithful make their thoughts match what they say and hear, and cooperate with divine grace;
b. but also external, that is, they express their inner participation through their gestures, outward bearing, acclamations, responses, and song.

Despite these and other positive elements in *Musicam Sacram*, the document remained something of an interim statement and, given the many uncertainties about how the reforms would unfold, it was by necessity somewhat ambiguous on key musical and liturgical questions of the day. As Anthony Ruff has demonstrated,[4] for example, while the document allows inherited musical forms such as chant to be employed in the liturgy, such chants cannot simply be used as they were previously. Rather, the ancient chants must now meet the new functional criterion articulated for liturgical music in CSL: "sacred music is to be considered the more holy, the more closely connected

4. This assessment of *Musicam Sacram* follows Ruff's thoughts from *Sacred Music and Liturgical Reform: Treasures and Transformations* (Chicago: Hillenbrand Books, 2007), 353–57.

it is with the liturgical action" (no. 112).[5] Furthermore, while *Musicam Sacram* does affirm the primacy of Gregorian Chant found in CSL, it seems to suggest that the use of Gregorian Chant is limited to Latin celebrations, which posed significant questions about the role of chant when the liturgy was celebrated in the vernacular. *Musicam Sacram* also upholds the importance of what CSL called the "treasury of sacred music" (no. 114), but such a treasury seems to include not only congregational music but even new musical compositions and forms under this umbrella term.

For these and other reasons, while *Musicam Sacram* did provide helpful directions it did not resolve many of the musical questions stirred up by the liturgical reforms. In the United States it was to fall to the US bishops and their various documents on music and liturgy to offer clarifications and directions for answering some of these questions.

The United States Bishops' Music Advisory Board

Within two months of the promulgation of *Musicam Sacram* the US bishops were taking steps that would eventually give rise to their first document on musical liturgy, *The Place of Music in Eucharistic Celebrations* (PMEC). In some ways the US bishops were remotely prepared for such an action because of developments that had taken place long before the convening of Vatican II. Already in 1917 they had established the National Catholic War Council to coordinate the activities of Roman Catholics during World War I, and in 1919 they created its permanent successor, renamed the National Catholic Welfare Council, with a permanent secretariat in Washington DC. Because of a dispute with the Vatican that almost led to the suppression of this organization, in 1922 the body was renamed the National Catholic Welfare *Conference* (NCWC).[6] In 1965 Vatican II's decree on bishops, *Christus Dominus* ("Christ the Lord"), affirmed the value of episcopal conferences and strongly encouraged that all "the bishops of each country or region would meet regularly" (no. 37). While it was not

5. This and subsequent translations are from *Vatican Council II: The Basic Sixteen Documents*, by Austin Flannery, OP (Dublin: Costello Publishing Company, Inc., 1996). Used with permission.

6. See the records of the American Catholic History Research Center and University Archives at http://libraries.cua.edu/achrcua/ncwcogs.html (accessed 30 April 2008).

explicitly mentioned, some contend that the National Catholic Welfare Conference was the model behind this image of conciliar governance.[7] After Vatican II the US bishops reorganized the NCWC into the National Conference of Catholic Bishops (NCCB) and its parallel secretariat, the United States Catholic Conference (USCC).

Even before the name change to USCC in 1966, the US bishops had already established their own national liturgical commission. The 1950s had been a time of much liturgical renewal, such as the reform of the Easter Vigil (1951) and of the Holy Week liturgies (1955). As Frederick McManus[8] reports it, these reforms were addressed on an ad hoc basis by the bishops, who had no liturgical commission or other organization in place at the time to implement these rites in the United States.[9] To remedy this situation the bishops proposed in November of 1957 to create a national episcopal liturgical commission, and in September of 1958 an "Episcopal Committee for the Liturgical Apostolate" was approved by the bishops, with Archbishop Joseph Ritter of St. Louis as the first chair.[10]

Under Archbishop John Dearden of Detroit (d. 1988)—who twice chaired (1959–60 and 1963–66) what came to be known in 1966 as the Bishops' Committee on the Liturgy (BCL)—the bishops appointed their first "Music Advisory Board" in the spring of 1965. The group convened for its inaugural meeting 4–5 May 1965 in Detroit, during which Rembert Weakland[11] (b. 1927) was elected chair of the new

7. Timothy Dolan, "The Conciliar Tradition of the American Hierarchy," 2004 Erasmus Lecture, available at http://www.archmil.org/resources/ShowResource.asp?ID=1531 (accessed 30 April 2008).

8. Monsignor Frederick McManus, JCD (d. 2005), was on the faculty of the Catholic University of America from 1959 until 1993, where he successively served as professor of canon law, dean of the School of Canon Law, vice provost and dean of graduate studies (1974–83), and academic vice president (1983–85). A *peritus* ("expert") at Vatican II, he maintained a long association with the Bishops' Committee on the Liturgy, serving as its first executive secretary (1965–75) and continuing as advisor to that committee; he was also one of the founders of the International Committee (later "Commission") on English in the Liturgy, an organization he served in various roles until the late 1990s.

9. Frederick R. McManus, ed., *Thirty Years of Liturgical Renewal: Statements of the Bishops' Committee on the Liturgy* (Washington, DC: National Conference of Catholic Bishops, 1987), 5. Much of my retelling of this history relies on McManus's work.

10. Ibid., 6–7.

11. Weakland was a doctoral candidate in musicology at Columbia University at the time; he completed the PhD in 2000. Archabbot of Latrobe Abbey (1963), he was elected Abbot Primate of the Benedictine Confederation (1967–77), and then appointed

board with Richard Schuler[12] as its secretary.[13] Father Frederick Mc-Manus, then executive director of what soon was to be known as the Bishops' Committee on the Liturgy, was the official liaison with the bishops. Archbishop Weakland recalls how crucial the Detroit meeting was for the future direction of the group,[14] as it demonstrated how committed the US bishops were to liturgical and musical reforms. Some, for example, thought that the decision at Vatican II to allow the vernacular (CSL, no. 36) was more about Africa and Asia than it was for the United States and Europe, but many of the US bishops were quite insistent about moving ahead quickly with this change to the vernacular and were especially eager to expand the use of the vernacular beyond the modest range envisioned by the council.[15]

Early evidence of widespread episcopal support for this vernacular move is detectable in the actions of the US bishops at their November 1963 meeting. Just a month before the promulgation of CSL they voted 130 to 5 to "'avail themselves of the vernacular concessions' made by the council" and by a vote of 127 to 7 "authorized the commission 'to prepare translations for interim use.'"[16] Archbishop Dearden, along

Archbishop of Milwaukee (1977–2002). Pope Paul VI had earlier appointed him as Consultor to (1964) and then a member of (1968) the Commission for Implementing the CSL.

12. Monsignor Richard Schuler was a priest of the Archdiocese of St. Paul-Minneapolis. He held the PhD in musicology from the University of Minnesota (1963), taught music and theology at the college of St. Thomas, and was pastor of St. Agnes Church from 1969 to 2001. He died in 2007. He was a founder of the Church Music Association of America (1964), affiliated with the *Consociatio Internationalis Musicae Sacrae* discussed below. He served on the board until December of 1966, as reported in his "Chronicle of the Reform: Catholic Music in the 20th century," in *Cum Angelis Canere: Essays on Sacred Music and Pastoral Liturgy in Honour of Richard J. Schuler*, ed. Robert A. Skeris (St. Paul, MN: Catholic Church Music Associates, 1990), online at http://www .musicasacra.com/pdf/chron.pdf (accessed 4 March 2008), 22, n. 18.

13. Other members of the board were J. Robert Carroll, Richard B. Curtin, Louise Cuyler, Francis J. Guentner, Paul Hume, Theodore Marier, C. Alexander Peloquin, Robert Snow, and Eugene Walsh, as reported by Schuler in "Chronicle of the Reform," 21.

14. Author's interview with Archbishop Rembert Weakland OSB (4 April 2008); unless otherwise noted, subsequent material from Weakland is drawn from this interview as well.

15. "But since the use of the vernacular, whether in the Mass, the administration of the sacraments, or in other parts of the liturgy, may frequently be of great advantage to the people, a wider use may be made of it, especially in readings, directives and in some prayers and chants" (CSL, no. 36).

16. McManus, *Thirty Years of Liturgical Renewal*, 11.

with Archbishop Paul Hallinan of Atlanta (d. 1968), who served first as secretary and then as chair of the BCL after Dearden, spearheaded this movement. According to Weakland, they and others continued to pressure Pope Paul VI (d. 1978) to enlarge the use of the vernacular in the Mass.

A further sign of this progressive leadership among the US bishops was the position publicly taken by then Archabbot Weakland at the 1966 meeting of the *Consociatio Internationalis Musicae Sacrae* ("International Society for Sacred Music"). This "more conservative" organization[17] with strong German ties received papal approval on the Feast of St. Cecilia in 1962 and planned its first congress in the United States in conjunction with the Fifth International Church Music Congress, spread between Chicago and Milwaukee, in 1966. The apparent hope of the *Consociatio* was to win the support of American leadership in music and liturgy for its more conservative approach, which held, for example, that active participation was "primarily one of active listening."[18] Weakland reports that he had not intended to attend that meeting until he received a telephone call from Cardinal Dearden. Along with other US bishops, Dearden had aligned himself with a more progressive musical-liturgical view shared by many French and Italian bishops and reflected in the organization *Universa Laus*,[19] whose first president was Jesuit liturgist and composer Joseph Gelineau (d. 2008). At Dearden's request, Weakland went to the meeting and caucused with all the Americans present, asking: "Do you want to go down in history as the group that banned any kind of evolution?"[20] The outcome of this caucusing was a series of counter-resolutions

17. Ruff, *Sacred Music and Liturgical Reform*, 361.
18. Ibid., 365.
19. This is an "international study group for liturgical singing and instrumental music, formally constituted at Lugano, Switzerland in April 1966, based on a group of European liturgists and musicologists that had first started meeting in 1962 (though some of its members had been working together for a decade before that). The initial object was to support the work of those charged with presenting and then implementing the liturgical reforms of the Second Vatican Council; some of its members were in fact *periti* at the Council. The first trio of presidents were Joseph Gelineau (France), Erhard Quack (Germany) and Luigi Agustoni (Italian-speaking Switzerland). Other distinguished names present at the first formal meeting of the association included Helmut Hucke, Bernard Huijbers, David Julien and René Reboud." This summary by Paul Inwood appears on the homepage of Universa Laus at http://www.universalaus.org/gb/ULGBHistory.htm (accessed 15 September 2008).
20. Weakland interview.

from the United States to those proposed by the leadership of the *Consociatio*. In the end none of the resolutions passed and in the words of Weakland, "the *Consociatio* went home without anything in their pockets."[21] The irony was that at the time Weakland was president of the Church Music Association of America (CMAA), the United States affiliate of the *Consociatio*. Not surprisingly, he was "unelected" from that position at CMAA's meeting at the end of the 1966 congress.

The Crafting of a Document

Underlying Issues

When the Music Advisory Board first gathered in May of 1965, Rome had not yet granted permission to celebrate the Liturgy of the Hours in the vernacular—something that did not occur until 1967. While that struggle loomed in the distance, the bishops' Music Advisory Board decided they needed to move forward by shaping a document limited to a consideration of the role of music in the eucharistic liturgy. Thus one distinctive difference between PMEC and its successors was this intentionally narrowed focus.

There were several issues to be addressed in this new document. One was the newly developing roles of the psalmist and cantor within eucharistic liturgy in the United States. Since the 1950s, Joseph Gelineau had been both writing about the role of the psalmist and providing highly influential settings of psalms and canticles that placed the psalmist at the center of the musical dialogue.[22] There is a technical difference between a "psalmist," who in ancient Christian practice rendered only the psalms in worship,[23] and the more generic term "cantor" for the person who in the medieval church intoned and led a variety of chants and in contemporary parlance is more simply a

21. Ibid.

22. E.g., his *24 psaumes et un cantique* (Paris: Cerf, 1953), and *53 psaumes et 4 cantiques* (Paris: Cerf, 1954). These publications were the result of a larger collaborative effort with Raymond J. Tournay and Raymond Schwab, who reworked the Psalter of the Jerusalem Bible for singing. The result was the *Psautier de la Bible de Jérusalem* and the recording *Psaumes*, which won the Gran Prix de L'Academie Charles-Cros in 1953.

23. See my "The Cantor in Historical Perspective," *Worship* 56 (1982): 194–213. Gelineau's foundational work on this topic was submitted as his doctoral thesis, *"Antiphona. Recherches sur les formes liturgiques de la psalmodie dans les Églises syriennes des IVème et Vème siècles"* (Paris: Institut Catholique, 1960), under the direction of Louis Bouyer.

singer or leader of song. Sometimes in French this more generic leader is called the *animateur liturgique* ("liturgical animator"), to distinguish this role from that of the psalmist. PMEC does not mention the "psalmist," but speaks of the "cantor" four times, especially in its discussion of "role differentiation" under "liturgical judgment," where it notes that "special attention should be paid to the role of cantor."[24]

Another central issue was the new emphasis on active participation and an understanding of the role of the congregation beyond that of active listening: no longer as consumers of another's music but now musical "subjects" in the liturgy.[25] There were several consequences of this new emphasis. One was what some perceived to be an underplaying of the role of the choir or schola, which in the preconciliar period was the main musical voice in many communities.[26] With such strong emphasis on the active participation of the people—CSL uses some of it most forceful language on this topic[27]—attention seemed to tilt away from the vocal centrality of the choir. Even CSL provides a somewhat mixed message about the choir, noting that choirs must be "diligently developed" but then going on to stress that when (Gregorian) chant is used in the liturgy, pastors must do their best to ensure that "the whole body of the faithful may be able to take that active part which is rightly theirs" (no. 114). Many musicians and liturgists came to believe that the choir's main purpose was the enhancement of congregational song, a position that could be construed

24. III. C. 2. b; III. C. 2. c is a paragraph on the "cantor," the only musical-ministerial role that receives an entire paragraph in this document. The "celebrant" also has a paragraph on the proper declamation of the Eucharistic Prayer (IV. B. 1. b).

25. For a summary of this development see David Power and Catherine Vincie, "Theological and Pastoral Reflections," in *A Commentary on the General Instruction of the Roman Missal*, ed. Edward Foley and others (Collegeville: Liturgical Press, 2007), 51–55.

26. While it is one of the more polemical sections of an otherwise fine volume, Ruff provides an overview of some of this struggle in his chapter 18: "Problem Area II: The Role of the Choir" (Ruff, *Sacred Music and Liturgical Reform*, 382–416).

27. "It is *very much the wish* of the church that all the faithful should be led to take that full, conscious, and active part in liturgical celebrations which is *demanded* by the very nature of the liturgy, and to which the Christian people, 'a chosen race, a royal priesthood, a holy nation, a redeemed people' (1 Pet 2:9, 4-5) *have a right* and to which *they are bound* by reason of their Baptism.

"In the restoration and development of the sacred liturgy the full and active participation by all the people is *the paramount concern*, for it is the *primary*, indeed the *indispensable source* from which the faithful are to derive the true Christian spirit" (no. 14, emphasis added).

from a 1966 statement of the US bishops that seems to put the singing of the choir alone in second place, behind this enhancement role.[28]

A final key concern related to active participation and the role of the choir in the Eucharist was balancing the "pastorally acceptable" with the "aesthetically pleasing." Rembert Weakland remembers that this was the most difficult issue of all. On the one hand, the church had a long tradition of singing Gregorian Chant, the polyphony of Palestrina (d. 1594) and de Lassus (d. 1594), as well as the Masses of Mozart (d. 1791) and Haydn (d. 1809)—the last two particularly in the German-speaking countries. On the other hand, this music was written for specialists[29] and ordinarily put the assembly into a primarily "listening mode" of participation, a stance unacceptable to many US bishops and their representatives on the Music Advisory Board.

An early struggle highlighting this tension was the 1965 debate within the committee about the introduction of more contemporary forms of music, especially for high school and college students. A key instigation for this development was a presentation by Fr. Godfrey Diekmann (d. 2002)[30] in April of 1965 to the National Catholic Educational Association entitled "Liturgical Renewal and the Student Mass." In this speech Diekmann advocated the use of guitars and "folk music" in eucharistic liturgies with students. A similar proposal was subsequently considered by the Music Advisory Board at their 1966 meeting in Chicago. A contentious debate ensued, resulting in what Richard Schuler reports was a "much modified" statement.[31] While this very brief document (less than 250 words) on "The Use of Music for Special Groups" never mentions guitars or "folk" music, it does demonstrate

28. "At times, the choir, within the congregation of the faithful and as part of it, will assume the role of leadership, while at other times, it will retain its own distinctive ministry. This means that the choir will lead the people in sung prayer by alternating or reinforcing the sacred song of the congregation or by enhancing it with the addition of a musical elaboration. At other times . . . the choir alone will sing works whose musical demands enlist and challenge its competence." US Bishops' statement, 18 April 1966. Quoted in McManus, *Thirty Years of Liturgical Renewal*, 43.

29. On the development of the Gregorian "propers" by specialists for specialists see James McKinnon, *The Advent Project: The Later-Seventh-Century Creation of the Roman Mass Propers* (Berkeley: University of California Press, 2000), especially 356–74.

30. A monk of St. John's Abbey in Collegeville, Diekmann was editor of *Orate Fratres* (later *Worship*), a consultant to the Pontifical Liturgical Preparatory Commission for Vatican II, *peritus* at the Council (1963–65), and a founder of the International Commission on English in the Liturgy (ICEL). See Kathleen Hughes, *The Monk's Tale* (Collegeville, MN: Liturgical Press, 1991).

31. Schuler, "Chronicle of the Reform," 22.

an openness to different styles and idioms "which help to make the liturgy meaningful" to "different groupings of the faithful." It further admits that "the choice of music which is meaningful to [youth of high school or college age] should be considered valid and purposeful."[32] While sections of this text were not explicitly incorporated into PMEC, these pastoral sentiments seem to pervade the document. Specific considerations of various "styles" of music would reappear in MCW.

"The Place of Music in Eucharistic Celebrations"

At its meeting at Kansas City, Missouri, on 1–2 December 1966 the Music Advisory Board underwent significant personnel change.[33] Father Eugene Walsh (d. 1989),[34] who had been on the Advisory Board since its inception, was given a key role by the reformed board in shaping PMEC; Archbishop Weakland also remembers Maryknoll Fr. Robert Ledogar[35] as playing an important role in the crafting of this document. By the end of 1967 Walsh had overseen the writing of a relatively short document (ca. 4600 words), with few footnotes, that according to Monsignor McManus would have more impact than any other statement of the BCL.[36] The statement was approved by the BCL in late 1967 and published in 1968. The basic outline of the document is:

32. "The Use of Music for Special Groups," in McManus, *Thirty Years of Liturgical Renewal*, 44.

33. According to Schuler, "the following were retired from the Music Advisory Board: Monsignor Curtin, Fr. Schuler, Fr. McNaspy, Louise Cuyler, Alexander Peloquin and Paul Hume. In their places the Archbishop appointed Fr. Paul Byron, Fr. John Cannon and Fr. Robert Ledogar. Also added were Dennis Fitzpatrick, Haldan Tompkins and Richard Feliciano" (Schuler, "Chronicle of The Reform," 22 n. 18). Schuler later offers his interpretation that the intention here was to render the committee "free of members who would likely oppose the projected statement" (ibid., 33).

34. Walsh was a Sulpician priest who was a student of the violin, had studied voice as a seminarian, and was the seminary's choir director before his ordination in 1938. Awarded an MA in Philosophy and then a PhD in Theology (1945) from the Catholic University of America, he first taught music, Latin, and English at St. Charles College in Baltimore, and after the PhD taught philosophy of education and music as well as theology at the Sulpician "Paca Street" Seminary in Baltimore. He became rector at Theological College in Washington DC in 1968, then in 1971 moved to a faculty position at that school, where he assisted with the pastoral program and taught courses in liturgy and music.

35. At the time Ledogar was professor of Liturgy and Sacramental Theology at Maryknoll Seminary in New York. For more on Fr. Ledogar, see below, chap. 2, n. 12.

36. McManus, *Thirty Years of Liturgical Renewal*, 92.

[Introduction] 1–3[37]

I. The Theology of Celebration

II. The Principle of Pastoral Celebration

    A. Good signs: simple and comprehensible

        1. In themselves

        2. In articulation and proportion

        3. In manner of celebration

    B. Four criteria:

        1. Humanly attractive experience

        2. Degree of solemnity

        3. Nature of congregation

        4. Available resources

III. The Place of Music in the Celebration

    A. The amount of singing will vary according to the circumstances

    B. Music serves the expression of faith

    C. There are three judgments to be made

        1. The musical judgment

        2. The liturgical judgment

            a. Text requirements

            b. Role differentiation

            c. The cantor

        3. The pastoral judgment

        4. A further problem (the problem of faith)

IV. Application of the Principles of Celebration to the Eucharist

    A. The Liturgy of the Word

        1. Service of the Word

            a. Purpose

            b. Consists of

            c. Recommendations for

                i. Hearing of God's word

                ii. Psalms

                iii. "Thanks be to God"

---

37. Unlike subsequent documents, PMEC was not sequentially ordered with numbered paragraphs but organized with a standard outline form, e.g., I. A. 1. a. i., etc.

        iv. Creed

        v. Prayer of the Faithful

  2. The Entrance Rite

    a. Quite secondary to the proclamation of the Word

    b. Should create an atmosphere of celebration

    c. Consists of

    d. Recommendations for

        i.   Musical settings of the entrance song

        ii. Confession prayers

        iii. Reciting the "Lord, Have Mercy" and "Glory to God"

        iv. The Prayer (collect)

B. The Liturgy of the Eucharist

  1. The Eucharistic Prayer

    a. The Eucharistic Prayer is praise and thanksgiving

    b. Quality of the celebration more dependent on the celebrant

    c. Preparatory Rite (offertory)

        i.   Purpose

        ii. Consists of

        iii. Recommendations for

            (a) Bringing the gifts in procession

            (b) The prayer over the gifts

            (c) Secondary elements

            (d) Procession can be accompanied by song

  2. Communion rite

    a. Unity of the Body

    b. Parts that comprise the communion rite

    c. Recommendations for celebration

        i.   Lord's Prayer

        ii. Lamb of God

        iii. Communion Song

    d. The dismissal rite

        i.   Purpose

        ii. One continuous action

        iii. Closing hymn

Although PMEC cites *Musicam Sacram* seven times, it is clear that this very "American" document, published less than a year after the appearance of *Musicam Sacram*, is exceedingly different in tone and content from its Vatican counterpart. For example, this groundbreaking statement on music stressed the importance of articulating a theology of celebration before turning to any distinctive musical concerns. Thus it is here that we first find insights such as: "To celebrate the liturgy means to do the action, or to perform the sign, in such a way that its full meaning and import shine forth in the most clear and compelling fashion" (II. A.) or the powerful: "Good celebrations foster and nourish faith; poor celebrations weaken and destroy faith" (Introduction).

There is a great deal of emphasis on the human and "humanly attractive," symbolized in what must have been a shocking phrase for 1968: "Music, more than any other resource, makes a celebration of the liturgy an attractive human experience" (III). It is also here that we not only for the first time discover the inventive articulation of the threefold "musical, liturgical, and pastoral" judgments but also a special pastoral emphasis in liturgical renewal. Particularly noteworthy is this early paragraph in the 1968 document:

> . . . it is clear that all sacramental celebrations are in themselves pastoral. Liturgies of a more elaborate form . . . must not be less pastoral than that of any parish. The pastoral purpose always governs the use and function of every element of the celebration. (II. B. 4)

A subtle turn in this document is the tendency to consider elements in the eucharistic liturgy according to their liturgical significance rather than simply according to their chronological occurrence within the rite. Thus, for example, when considering "the application of the principles of celebration to the Eucharist" the document does not begin with the "Entrance Rite" (IV. A. 2) but with the more important "Service of the Word" (IV. A. 1); similarly, it turns to the "Eucharistic Prayer" (IV. B. 1) before providing instructions about the "Preparatory Rite" (IV. B. 1. c). This intentional and inventive structuring of the document well models an early and important principle articulated under the rubric of "proportion," that is, "What is of lesser importance should appear so; what is of greater importance should clearly emerge as such" (II. A. 2). This wise statement presumes a particular pastoral strategy for selecting liturgical music that is still often underutilized or ignored, namely, that the reformed rites, with their clear distinctions between primary and secondary elements, need to be planned from the "inside out" rather than from "beginning to end." The former strategy holds more promise for crafting a musical contour that respects the intrinsic ebb and flow of the eucharistic liturgy.

As previously noted, it is difficult to offer any definitive assessment of PMEC until one looks at the music documents from the US bishops that followed. It is only after that exercise that we will be able to appreciate the unique and enduring pastoral vision that marks this breakthrough document. Thus it is now appropriate that we turn to the first reincarnation of PMEC, *Music in Catholic Worship.*

2 A Landmark Document

The Background

While decades separate the other music documents of the US bishops, barely four years intervened between the publication of *The Place of Music in Eucharistic Celebrations* (PMEC) and *Music in Catholic Worship* (MCW). While that span may appear to be a very brief period of time, it is useful to remember that this was an era in which Roman Catholic liturgy—along with many other institutions in Western societies—was undergoing rapid and radical change. In 1969, for example, Rome published the long-awaited new *Order of Mass* along with the first edition of the *General Instruction of the Roman Missal*.[1] Within a year of those publications Pope Paul VI (d. 1978) promulgated the official edition (Latin = *editio typica*) of the Roman Missal. That same year he also promulgated the official edition of the Lectionary along with its substantial Introduction (Latin = *Proemium*).

Liturgy in the Vernacular

All of these documents, of course, were published in Latin. Translation was the task of the International Commission on English in the Liturgy (ICEL), established in 1963 by bishops from ten English-speaking conferences around the world. This preemptive action was taken by visionary bishops in anticipation of the Constitution on the Sacred Liturgy, promulgated in December of that same year, that would allow the use of the vernacular in the liturgy. The English lectionary—which

1. To date there have been five subsequent editions of the *General Instruction of the Roman Missal* (1970, 1972, 1975, 1982, and 2002).

only required new translations of the introduction, titles, summaries, and some antiphons—appeared in 1970. The process for translating the Roman Missal, however, was much more arduous. While a provisional translation, under the auspices of the National Conference of Catholic Bishops (NCCB), did appear in May of 1972, a complete English translation of the Roman Missal (soon to be known in English as the "Sacramentary") was not approved by the NCCB until November of 1973 and subsequently confirmed by Rome in 1974. With the appearance of these Latin texts and then their English translations, pastors and musicians alike were confronted with new terminology, unfamiliar liturgical elements, and structural changes that were almost as confounding as they were exciting. The singular "Canon of the Mass" was now replaced by multiple "Eucharistic Prayers." The complex liturgical unit known as the "Offertory" was supplanted by a much simpler "Preparation of the Gifts and Table." The "gradual" and "tract" were transformed into the "chants between the readings," and everywhere there were "acclamations." Father William Bauman, a priest from the diocese of Kansas City-Saint Joseph and then chair of the music subcommittee of the FDLC, relates: "I remember when Bishop Helmsing[2] gave his Latin copy of the new Mass to me in the summer of 1969. I sat down and translated it for the priests of our diocese . . . and I kept running into this word 'acclamations.' We had no idea what an acclamation was!" Amazingly, what we take for granted was almost like a liturgical "moonscape" to those pioneers of the reform.

The "Liturgical" Publishing Industry

Another phenomenon that quickly and unexpectedly developed after the advent of PMEC was what was soon to become a burgeoning music publishing industry in the United States. Even before the Second Vatican Council, American publishers were issuing predominantly English-language hymnals. As early as 1955 Omer Westendorf (d. 1998), who in 1950 had founded the World Library of Sacred Music in Cincinnati, Ohio,[3] published the influential hymnal first called

2. Bishop Charles Herman Helmsing (d. 1993) was Bishop of Kansas City-Saint Joseph from 1962 until 1977.
3. The World Library of Sacred Music was eventually purchased by the J. S. Paluch Company in 1971 and is now a subsidiary of that company, known as World Library Publications or WLP.

People's Hymnal (1955). This groundbreaking work, rechristened as the *People's Mass Book* in 1961 and now in its eighth incarnation,[4] contained a significant amount of English hymnody. In the following year the Liturgical Press published *Our Parish Prays and Sings*, followed a year later by *Book of Sacred Song*.

After the Constitution on the Sacred of Liturgy was promulgated in 1963 the amount of publishing of liturgical music in English—especially in the new idiom of "folk" music[5] popularized in the early 1960s—grew exponentially. The undisputed leader in this new idiom was a fledgling publishing organization known as The Friends of the English Liturgy (abbreviated as FEL), which in 1966 introduced the wildly popular *Hymnal for Young Christians*. While the same organization would go on to produce two subsequent editions of that hymnal, none was as well received or influential as the original. Symptomatic of its influence was the inclusion of the song "And They'll Know We are Christians by Our Love," by Peter Scholtes. Decades later, liturgical historian James White commented that at one time this liturgical song was "almost inescapable at Mass."[6]

While not necessarily wanting to control the "liturgical" publishing industry, Roman Catholic leadership was interested in having an influence on it. For example, as Fr. William Bauman has documented,[7] in 1972 the FDLC had proposed the development of a national hymnal

---

4. According to Alan Hommerding at WLP, apart from the reprinting, editions with diocesan supplements, and different versions of the same edition, there appear to be eight "editions" of this publication: *People's Hymnal* 1955; *People's Mass Book* 1961, 1964, 1966, 1970, 1975, 1984, and 2003.

5. According to the standards set by "academics" this actually was not "folk" music. In 1955, for example, the International Folk Music Council adopted the following provisional definition of folk music: "Folk music is music that has been submitted to the process of oral transmission. It is the product of evolution, and is dependent on the circumstances of continuity, variation and selection. The term can therefore be applied to music that has been evolved from rudimentary beginnings by a community uninfluenced by art music; and it can also be applied to music which has originated with an individual composer, and has subsequently been absorbed into the unwritten, living tradition of a community. But the term does not cover a song, dance, or tune that has been taken over readymade and remains unchanged. It is the fashioning and refashioning of the music by the community that gives it its folk character." See Maud Karpeles, "Definitions of Folk Music," *Journal of the International Folk Music Council* 7 (1955): 6–7, at 6.

6. James White, *Roman Catholic Worship: Trent to Today* (Collegeville, MN: Liturgical Press, 2003), 147.

7. William Bauman, "The Birth of a Hymnal," *Musart* 26, no. 3 (1974): 6–8; also see his "The National Hymnal is Dead," *Pastoral Music* 1, no. 3 (1977): 20–21.

containing, among other things, five hundred songs along with musical settings of the Psalms and antiphons for the responsorial songs. While the proposal was already dead by the Spokane meeting of the FDLC in 1974, the push for a national hymnal symbolized just how important liturgical music publishing was becoming for Roman Catholic liturgy in the United States during the early 1970s.

The Apparent Divide

A widely employed maxim from the 1980s is that "perception is reality." While there has been a serious expenditure of energies—especially from philosophy and some branches of the social sciences—to debunk this axiom, there is yet some enduring and documentable truth about it. In the volatile economy late in the first decade of the twenty-first century, for example, many professional economists admitted that even though the United States economy did not initially meet the textbook definition of recession, that data was "trumped" by the perception of many American citizens that the economy was actually in recession.[8]

While there were virtually no social-scientific studies of liturgical-musical tastes and opinions in the 1960s, 1970s, and 1980s, there was still a documentable *perception* that the period after Vatican II witnessed a growing divide between the "musicians" and the "liturgists." While in some ways this caricature is a bit simplistic, since many of the so-called liturgists were very gifted and even celebrated musicians,[9] nonetheless there were exceedingly well trained and celebrated musicians and composers who occupied prominent positions at important churches and cathedrals in the United States in the 1960s and 1970s.[10] The presence and influence of "liturgists" was, on the other

8. Jeff Poor, "Perception Trumps Reality with Recession: Business correspondent Ali Velshi admits how people 'feel' is more important than economic fundamentals," Business and Media Institute, 18 October 2007, http://www.businessandmedia.org/articles/2007/20071018181509.aspx (accessed 7 July 2008).

9. Joseph Gelineau (d. 2008) is probably the most famous example here: while he held no degree in music and his doctorate from the Institut Catholique was in theology and he served as a theological *peritus* ("expert") at the Second Vatican Council, he is most celebrated for his musical compositions. So is he a "liturgist" or a "musician"? Maybe both, or maybe the categories do not do justice here.

10. For example, Dr. Mario Salvador was the longtime organist and choir director at the cathedral in St. Louis (1940–92); Paul Koch was organist and choirmaster at

hand, much more circumscribed. Advanced degrees in liturgy were a novelty and did not generally exist until the 1960s,[11] and most of the leading figures in the US liturgical movement had little formal training in liturgy.[12]

One of the growing concerns in this climate was the possible estrangement of the more classically trained organists, choirmasters, and composers serving the Roman Catholic Church in the United States during the mid-twentieth century. This was especially true in light of the explosion of liturgical compositions modeled on contemporary exemplars that were widely disseminated across the pop music scene in the United States and beyond. Innumerable composers, for example, wrote for single voice with guitar accompaniment in (often poor) imitation of Woody Guthrie (d. 1967) and Pete Seeger (b. 1919). I know of at least one celebrated example, who was one of the most published and sung liturgical musicians in the Roman Catholic Church in the United States, who could not even read music, and dictated his works into tape recorders for transcription by others. In light of the disparity not only between established musicians and newly minted "liturgists," but also between classically trained and well respected musicians and upstart "folk musicians," it is little wonder that the Music Advisory Board of the Bishops' Committee on the Liturgy would have the contentious debate we chronicled in the previous

---

Pittsburgh's St. Paul Cathedral 1949–89; virtuoso Charles Courboin was organist at St. Patrick's Cathedral in New York 1943–73, and Robert Twynham was organist at the Cathedral of Mary our Queen in Baltimore 1961–98.

11. The first doctorate in liturgy from the Institut Catholique in Paris, for example, was awarded in 1964 to Robert Ledogar, whom we previously noted was an important hand in PMEC. The first doctorate in Sacred Liturgy (SLD) was conferred by the Pontifical Liturgical Institute (San Anselmo) in Rome in 1962 on Adaikalam Lourdes, under the direction of Cipriano Vagaggini, on "Pastoral and Liturgical Enrichment of the Tamil Marriage Ritual"; the first PhD in theology with a concentration in liturgy in the United States was awarded to my teacher Ralph Keifer from the University of Notre Dame in 1972. His dissertation, directed by Aidan Kavanagh, OSB, was entitled "Oblation in the First Part of the Roman Canon: An Examination of a Primitive Eucharistic Structure and Theology in Early Italian and Egyptian Sources." The earliest doctorate in "liturgy" seems to have been awarded from the theological faculty in Trier to John H. Miller, CSC, in 1955 under the direction of Balthasar Fischer (d. 1980). Miller's dissertation was entitled "The Relationship between Liturgical and Private Prayer in the Light of the Controversy of the last 50 Years."

12. E.g., as noted above, Monsignor McManus held a doctorate in canon law and Godfrey Diekmann's doctoral work was in patristics (see Kathleen Hughes, *The Monk's Tale* [Collegeville, MN: Liturgical Press, 1991], 52–54).

chapter. In this same vein, it is also important to recall that in many if not most parishes in the late 1960s and early 1970s there emerged a vast cohort of volunteer musicians, many enthusiastic to sing "And They'll Know We Are Christians" and its multiple siblings. Most of these volunteers were musically (and liturgically) untrained. Their gifts in leading congregations in singing the new liturgy were often marked more by enthusiasm than by any disciplined musicality.

Another Collaborative Document

Given the speed of the liturgical reforms in the late 1960s and early 1970s as well as pressures from the burgeoning publishing industry and the growing divisiveness between professional musicians—especially those serving at key cathedrals around the country—and a new breed of liturgists and volunteer musicians, the time seemed ripe for further instruction on liturgy and music. Ironically, the impetus for the rewrite and ultimate replacement of PMEC known as *Music in Catholic Worship* (MCW) apparently did not come from the US bishops or their committee on the liturgy, which had been so effective in producing PMEC. Rather, it came from the Federation of Diocesan Liturgical Commissions. The background for this organization is to be found in number 44 of CSL, which instructs that "competent territorial ecclesiastical" authorities should set up liturgical commissions. Many dioceses in the United States complied. From 1966 to 1968 the BCL hosted the chairs and secretaries of those commissions at a series of meetings. At the 1968 meeting there was first a suggestion and then a resolution from the floor that there should be an "advisory committee" to the BCL. That advisory committee became the FDLC in 1969, consisting of two representatives from each of the twelve regions, who became the original board of directors. In 1970 the FDLC adopted a constitution and bylaws and was formally established.[13]

Father William Bauman was vice president of the FDLC and chair of its subcommittee on the liturgy. Apparently committed to honoring the FDLC seriously as its "advisory committee," the bishops either asked the FDLC to produce the document or, more probably, seem to have borrowed a document the FDLC wrote on its own initiative. Bauman identifies himself primarily as the editor of the resulting

13. This history is drawn from the information supplied on the FDLC website at http://www.fdlc.org/FDLC_History.htm (accessed 14 August 2008).

document, whose main drafter appears to have been Fr. Patrick Collins, a priest, theologian, and accomplished musician from Peoria, Illinois. Another important editorial hand in the project was Fr. Larry Heiman. A chant specialist with a Doctorate in Sacred Music from Rome's Pontifical Institute of Sacred Music, Heiman was founder and longtime director of the Rensselaer Program of Church Music and Liturgy. Writing with few instructions and little direction from the bishops, this trio took PMEC as its starting point, repeating much of what was good in that original document but also greatly modifying and expanding it. Whereas, for example, PMEC had just a little over 4,600 words, MCW was over 50 percent longer, with almost 7,300 words. The final product was presented at a meeting of the BCL in which Bauman reports there were no substantial changes and just a few minor modifications introduced by the bishops and their staff.

An overview of the basic outline of the documents demonstrates both its similarities to and its differences from its predecessor.

I.   The Theology of Celebration [1–9]
II. Pastoral Planning for Celebration [10–22]
         The congregation [15–18]
         The occasion [19–20]
         The celebrant [21–22]
III. The Place of Music in the Celebration [23–41]
         Music serves the expression of faith [23–25]
         The musical judgment [26–29]
         The liturgical judgment [30–38]
             a. Structural requirements [31]
             b. Textual requirements [32]
             c. Role differentiation [33]
             d. The congregation [34]
             e. The cantor [35]
             f. The choir [36]
             g. The organist and other instrumentalists [37–38]
         The pastoral judgment [39–41]
IV. General Considerations of Liturgical Structure [42–49]
         The Introductory Rites [44]
         The Liturgy of the Word [45]
         The Preparation of the Gifts [46]

Comparing this with the outline of PMEC (see chap. 1 above), we can note some of the more significant structural, theological, and stylistic similarities and differences. First, both documents begin with statements about the "Theology of Celebration." Furthermore, the similarities in structure, theology, and even wording between the first nine paragraphs of MCW and the first four paragraphs of PMEC's section I, as well as the first nine paragraphs of section II, demonstrate why Frederick McManus and others refer to MCW as a "revised and expanded" version of PMEC.[14] In the following chart, *italics* indicate a language change or addition in the 1972 document.

PMEC	MCW
The Theology of Celebration: Good celebrations foster and nourish faith; poor celebrations weaken and destroy faith.	The Theology of Celebration
We are Christians because through the Christian community we have met Jesus Christ, heard his word of invitation, and responded to him in faith. We assemble together at Mass in order to speak our faith over again in community and, by speaking it, to renew and deepen it. We do not come together to meet Christ as if he were absent from the rest of our lives. We come together to deepen our awareness of, and commitment to, the action of His Spirit in the whole of our lives at every moment. We come together to acknowledge the work of the Spirit in us, to offer thanks, to celebrate.	1. A man is a Christian because through the Christian community he has met Jesus Christ, heard his word of invitation, and responded to him in faith. Christians *gather* at Mass *that they may hear and express our faith again in this assembly and, by expressing it,* renew and deepen it. 2. We do not come to meet Christ as if he were absent from the rest of our lives. We come together to deepen our awareness of, and commitment to, the action of his Spirit in the whole of our lives at every moment. We come together to acknowledge *the love of God poured out among us in* the work of the Spirit, *to stand in awe and praise.*
	3. *We are celebrating when we involve ourselves meaningfully in the thoughts, words, songs, and gestures of the worshiping community—when everything we do is wholehearted and authentic for us—when we mean the words and want to do what is done.*

14. Frederick R. McManus, ed., *Thirty Years of Liturgical Renewal: Statements of the Bishops' Committee on the Liturgy* (Washington, DC: National Conference of Catholic Bishops, 1987), 92.

PMEC	MCW
People in love make signs of love and celebrate their love for the dual purpose of expressing and deepening that love. We too must express in signs our faith in Christ and each other, our love for Christ and for each other, or they will die. We need to celebrate.	4. People in love make signs of love, *not only to* express their love *but also to* deepen *it. Love never expressed dies. Christians' love for Christ and for one another and Christians' faith in Christ and in each other must be expressed in the signs and symbols of celebration* or it will die
We may not feel like celebrating on this or that Sunday, even though we are called by the Church's law to do so. Our faith does not always permeate our feelings. But this is the function of signs in the Church: to give bodily expression to faith, to transform our fragile awareness of Christ's presence in the dark of our daily isolation into a joyful, integral experience of his liberating action in the solidarity of the celebrating community.	5. *Celebrations need not fail, even on a particular Sunday when our feelings do not match the invitation of Christ and his Church to worship.* Faith does not always permeate our feelings. But *the* signs *and symbols of worship can* give bodily expression to faith *as we celebrate. Our own faith is stimulated. We become one with others whose faith is similarly expressed. We rise above our own feelings to respond to God in prayer.*
From this it is clear that the manner in which the Church celebrates the liturgy has an effect on the faith of men. Good celebrations foster and nourish faith. Poor celebrations weaken and destroy faith.	6. *Faith grows when it is well expressed in celebration.* Good celebrations foster and nourish faith. Poor celebrations weaken and destroy it.
II. The Principle Of Pastoral Celebration: The primary goal of all celebration is to make a humanly attractive experience.	
A. Good signs: simple and comprehensible	
To celebrate the liturgy means to do the action, or to perform the sign, in such a way that its full meaning and import shine forth in the most clear and compelling	7. To celebrate the liturgy means to do the action or perform the sign in such a way that the full meaning and impact shine forth in clear and compelling fashion. *Since these*

PMEC	MCW
fashion. The signs of sacramental celebration are vehicles of communication and instruments of faith. They must be good signs, simple and comprehensible; they must be humanly attractive.	signs are vehicles of communication and instruments of faith, they must be simple and comprehensible. *Since they are directed to fellow human beings*, they must be humanly attractive. *They must be meaningful and appealing to the body of worshipers or they will fail to stir up faith and people will fail to worship the Father.*
In order to fulfill their purpose, liturgical actions must be genuine celebrations: in themselves, in articulation and proportion, in manner of celebration.	
1. In themselves: "The rites should be distinguished by a noble simplicity; they should be short, clear and unencumbered by useless repetition; they should be within the peoples' power of comprehension and normally should not require much explanation" (Constitution on the Liturgy, art. 34).	8. *The signs of celebration* should be short, clear, and unencumbered by useless repetition; they should be "within the people's powers of comprehension, and normally should not require much explanation." *If the signs need explanation to communicate faith, they will often be watched instead of celebrated.*
2. In articulation and proportion: Each part of the celebration should be clear in itself. (E.g., an entrance rite should clearly demonstrate by the elements that make it up and by the manner in which these are carried out in the celebration just what its purpose is.) Each part should be so articulated with the other parts that there emerges from the celebration the sense of a unified whole. What is of lesser importance should appear so; what is of greater importance should clearly emerge as such. (E.g., the	

PMEC	MCW
offertory procession, from its manner and length of celebration, should not appear to be of greater importance than the Canon.)	
3. In manner of celebration: Each sacramental action must be invested with the personal care, attention, and enthusiasm of those who carry it out. (E.g., when the celebrant greets the community, he should do so in a way indicating clearly that he knows what he is doing and that he really means to do it.)	9. *In true celebration* each *sign or* sacramental action will be invested with the personal *and prayerful faith*, care, attention, and enthusiasm of those who carry it out.

While the two documents use different styles for ordering the material, in the sense that PMEC employs a standard outline form in the document [I. A. 1. a. (1) and MCW uses the more familiar standard of continuously numbered paragraphs, this side-by-side comparison leaves no doubt as to the genealogy of MCW. Admittedly, while these opening paragraphs of the 1968 and 1972 documents are probably the most similar parallel sections of the two, they reveal some tendencies that would be apparent if we provided a complete comparison of the two documents in parallel columns. First, the earlier document has a tendency to insert more concrete examples, e.g., in much of II. A. 2 and then again in II. A. 3, where it provides a series of parenthetical "e.g.'s" about the entrance rite, the offertory procession, and the celebrant greeting the community. On the other hand, the 1972 document tends not only to expand certain principles but also to add new ones, for example, in its new paragraph 3.

Another place where there is a clear parallel between the two documents is in the previously mentioned judgments: musical, liturgical, and pastoral. While they are quite similar in substance, there are some notable differences here. First, we again see the tendency of MCW to expand considerably the discussion of the judgments. For example, it adds numbers 27 and 28 on the musical judgment, which have no parallel in the 1968 document. Furthermore, MCW adds a paragraph on "structural requirements" (no. 31), although it does echo some of the concern about the relative importance of each part of the celebration that the 1968 document took up in II. A. 2. Finally, under "role differentiation," MCW adds a paragraph on the congregation (no. 34), one on the choir (no. 36), and two on the organist and other instrumentalists (nos. 37–38).

A subtle but important distinction between PMEC and MCW regards the actual number of judgments to be made. PMEC is quite consistent in talking about the need for "three judgments" (e.g., II. C). MCW, on the other hand, introduces the topic by noting that "a three-fold judgment must be made: musical, liturgical, pastoral" (no. 25). It is not consistent in this regard, however, and in number 42 MCW will speak of "the three preceding judgments." While MCW does seem to have a more unitive vision of the convergence of these three—which is also the memory of some of its drafters—it is not exactly clear on the matter. This lack of clarity contributed to a perception among some in the following decades that these were three independent judgments, often arrived at by three different people (e.g., the musician, liturgist, and pastor), and were frequently competing judgments in which one voice eventually prevailed rather than three voices in a mutual dialogue leading to a consensus. This discrepancy received considerable attention in *The Milwaukee Symposia for Church Composers: A Ten-Year Report*,[15] which called for an integrated, single, multifaceted judgment (nos. 81–86). As we will discuss below, the 2007 document *Sing to the Lord* will also address this discrepancy by speaking of "three judgments: one evaluation" (no. 126).

There are many parallels between section IV in PMEC ("Application of the Principles of Celebration to the Eucharist") and section V in MCW ("Application of the Principles of Celebration to Music in Eucharistic Worship"). Since the lectionary, the *Ordo Missae*, and the *General Instruction of the Roman Missal* all appeared between these two documents, MCW included changes and acknowledged developments that were unknown to PMEC. For example, whereas PMEC will refer to the "epistle" (e.g., IV. A. 1. b), that term never occurs in MCW, which instead speaks about the "first lesson" or "first reading"

15. Sister Theophane Hytrek (d. 1992) conceived of the symposia as forums for dialogue between liturgists and composers. Cosponsored by Archbishop Weakland, the group convened in 1982, 1985, 1988, 1990, and 1992. The participants in the symposia varied somewhat from year to year, and the thirty-nine final signatories of the document were not the only ones who helped generate it. This author was the primary drafter of the document, conjointly published by the National Association of Pastoral Musicians in Washington DC and Liturgy Training Publications in Chicago, Illinois.

(both in no. 63). In general, MCW has a much more developed theology of the word, acknowledging it as one of the modes of Christ's presence (no. 45). MCW acknowledges the possibility of a sprinkling rite at the beginning of Mass (no. 44), which was unknown to PMEC and quite different from the *Asperges* in the Tridentine Rite, which technically occurred before Mass began.

MCW separates "Considerations of Liturgical Structure" (section IV, nos. 42–49) from "Application of the Principles of Celebration to Music in Eucharistic Worship" (section V, nos. 50–78). As a consequence, the material found in PMEC's section IV ("Application of the Principles of Celebration to the Eucharist") is scattered over these two sections and significantly expanded. Thus there is added attention in MCW to acclamations (e.g., no. 53), the Alleluia (no. 55), the Doxology to the Lord's Prayer, which did not exist prior to the 1969 *Ordo Missae* (no. 59), and the Lord's Prayer itself (no. 67). Furthermore, MCW adds a new category of "supplementary songs" (nos. 70–74), and addresses new patterns of singing (no. 75).

For the first time this document also addresses the issue of just compensation, both for musicians (no. 77) and for composers and publishers (no. 78), a testimony to the rise of a growing cadre of pastoral musicians and the burgeoning of the publishing industry. Finally, the document turns to worship music outside of Eucharist and introduces five short paragraphs on "Music in Sacramental Celebrations" (nos. 79–83).

Contributions and Controversies

The impact of MCW was relatively quick, eventually very widespread, and quite sustained. While clearly beholden to PMEC for many of its key insights and directions, MCW quickly outstripped its predecessor in terms of its availability, its catalytic role in sparking the musical-liturgical conversation, and its value as a study text and guide. The reasons for this expansive distribution and consumption are multiple. First, PMEC was never separately published and was more often distributed as a mimeographed text[16] or as typed excerpts, which were occasionally quoted or referenced in other documents or publications. Its primary published form was the useful but not widely distributed collection *Thirty Years of Liturgical Renewal*, edited

16. This is how this author first acquired the statement.

by Frederick McManus.[17] MCW, on the other hand, was published as a separate booklet in 1972 by the United States Catholic Conference and was widely purchased by pastors, musicians, liturgists, seminarians, and members of parish liturgy committees. It eventually found its way into very popular paperback collections of documents such as *The Liturgy Documents: A Parish Resource*.[18]

The document also received both scholarly and pastoral attention very early on. Already in mid-1973 Erik Routley was citing the document in an article in *Worship*,[19] something that would happen over seventy times in that distinguished journal over the next three decades. More popular pastoral publications such as *Pastoral Liturgy*,[20] *Folk Mass and Modern Liturgy, Musart*, and similar journals kept MCW front and center as liturgists and musicians struggled to give shape to musical liturgy during the mid-1970s.

It was especially the mushrooming of training days, workshops, and certificate programs for so many volunteer liturgists and musicians in the 1970s that contributed to the document's deep entrenchment in the pastoral musician's psyche. Here was a bridge document, accessible to people who had never negotiated the *General Instruction of the Roman Missal*, providing an apparently reasonable and understandable introduction to liturgical music from the Bishops' Committee on the Liturgy. Less arcane than *Musicam Sacram*, written in straightforward English prose, and applicable whether one's instrument was organ or guitar, MCW filled a void for those searching for a credible guide through the unexplored wilderness of liturgical music in the first decades after Vatican II. When the journal *Pastoral Music* was launched by the newly formed National Association of Pastoral Musicians it devoted an entire issue in each of its first four years of publication to MCW.[21]

There is also anecdotal information from other English-speaking countries that in the absence of their own indigenous documents on liturgical music MCW found some international currency. This appears

17. See above, n. 15.

18. First edited by Gabe Huck and published by Chicago's Liturgy Training Publications in 1980, this collection is currently in its fourth (2007) edition.

19. See his "Contemporary Catholic Hymnody in its Wider Setting," *Worship* 47, no. 6 (June–July, 1973): 322–37, at 333.

20. *Pastoral Liturgy* began as *Rite 70*, *Rite 80*, and *Rite 90* before returning to *Rite* in 2000 and *Pastoral Liturgy* in 2008.

21. *Pastoral Music* 1, no. 4 (April–May, 1977); 2, no. 2 (December–January, 1978); 3, no. 4 (April–May, 1979); and 4, no. 2 (December–January, 1980).

especially to be true in Australia, where multiple respondents from various dioceses noted the use of this document in their own teaching or writing. Even where the document itself was not specifically quoted, the "three liturgical judgments" were somewhat widely employed.[22]

As to its distinctive contributions to the dialogue, William Bauman would argue that a primary one was MCW's distinction between quality and musical style.[23] In the previously noted rift between more classically trained musicians and the growing number of "folk" musicians, there was the natural tendency to impose one's personal or professional standards on music crafted in a completely different genre. Taking this issue head on, MCW provided paragraph 28, which successively spoke of chant, polyphony, and "folk music" in the same context, disallowing any evaluation across styles:

> We do a disservice to musical values, however, when we confuse the judgment of music with the judgment of musical style. Style and value are two distinct judgments. Good music of new styles is finding a happy home in the celebrations of today. To chant and polyphony we have effectively added the chorale hymn, restored responsorial singing to some extent, and employed many styles of contemporary composition. Music in folk idiom is finding acceptance in eucharistic celebrations. We must judge value within each style.

Bauman has also expressed the view that MCW contributed mightily to ending the "four-hymn syndrome" at Mass, i.e., singing a hymn at the Entrance, "Offertory," Communion, and Dismissal. The document's emphasis on acclamations, the strong need to understand what was essential in the structure of the Mass (no. 42), and the continual reference to those things that were "primary" and those that were "secondary" (e.g., nos. 44, 45, and 46) lends credence to this view.

Father Patrick Collins, who had been present at the Fifth International Church Music Congress in 1966,[24] had a further contribution to

22. I am grateful to the Rev. Dr. Thomas Elich, director of the Liturgy Office for the Archdiocese of Brisbane and former national secretary of the National Liturgical Council, who solicited responses from colleagues in Hobart, Melbourne, Maitland-Newcastle, and Adelaide, as well as from the current national secretary.

23. The word "style" occurs fourteen times throughout the document, in a variety of different contexts, cumulatively giving the clear impression that different styles both of music and of celebration were appropriate to certain groups at certain times, suggesting a broad view of liturgical adaptation here.

24. See above, chap. 1, 15.

add. He believed that out of the 1966 conference, where many representatives of the United States disagreed with the perspectives of their European counterparts, there had come a determination on the part of some to craft a document that provided an "American" reading of the musical-liturgical reform at the time. Archbishop Weakland provides a useful nuance to this reading of the document when he recalls how close his thinking and that of other leaders in the United States was to that of Joseph Gelineau, Lucien Deiss, and other Europeans. Thus he concludes that MCW demonstrated the alliance between that document and the voice of *Universa Laus*, and the divergence between the document and the work of the *Consociatio*.

One point of contention in subsequent years would be the authority of the document, since it (like its predecessor) was not formally approved by the entire NCCB, but was approved and published by the BCL itself. Some thought this constituted an "end run" around the proper channels and diminished the magisterial weight of the document. Actually, the publication of documents by committees of the NCCB was commonplace in that era, e.g., the celebrated *Fulfilled in Your Hearing* (1982) was published by the Bishops' Committee on Priestly Life and Ministry. Furthermore, in 1983, on the tenth anniversary of the promulgation of the *Constitution on the Sacred Liturgy*, the NCCB issued a pastoral statement entitled "The Church at Prayer." In that document, approved in plenary session, the NCCB notes: ". . . our Committee on the Liturgy has issued statements which have been well received and proven very useful, especially *Music in Catholic Worship, Liturgical Music Today* and *Environment and Art in Catholic Worship*. The norms and guidelines of these documents should be followed by pastors and all those engaged in the liturgical arts."[25] Such a statement, with its language of norms and guidelines and "should be followed," seems to erase any suggestion that pastors, liturgists, and musicians were free to ignore MCW.

Summary

At the end of the previous chapter we indicated that it was difficult to assess adequately the import of PMEC without considering MCW, which a leader like Frederick McManus considered almost as two

25. National Conference of Catholic Bishops, *The Church at Prayer: A Holy Temple of the Lord* (Washington, DC: USCC, 1983), 23.

recensions of the same document, or what he called a "revision."[26] Much of the original spirit, musical sensitivity, and pastoral genius of PMEC shines through in MCW. MCW maintains many of PMEC's theological insights and honors while expanding its nascent theology of celebration. MCW incorporates and develops the key concepts of the tripartite judgment, though it does not forever settle the issue whether the intent was to set forth one or three judgments. We also saw how MCW incorporates many sections from PMEC's "Application of the Principles of Celebration to the Eucharist" into itself.

MCW does much more than PMEC and, as noted above, reflects the existence of a new *General Instruction of the Roman Missal*, Lectionary, and Sacramentary-in-process. At the same time, it does not seem an exaggeration to suggest that MCW actually pressed the essential insights of PMEC into the center of the United States musical-liturgical discussions and celebrations. Without such a smart and accessible rewrite-expansion it would be difficult to imagine how the insights of PMEC would ever have become part of contemporary musical-liturgical thinking among Roman Catholics in the United States.

Ironically, the value of MCW itself cannot be fully appreciated until we examine the two subsequent documents that could be understood as first safeguarding the contribution of MCW and then respectfully revisiting and revising it for a new generation of musicians, liturgists, and worshiping assemblies. Thus it is appropriate for us to turn the page once again and move on to *Liturgical Music Today*.

26. *Liturgical Music Today* makes a similar point when in its introduction it speaks of "*Music in Catholic Worship*, itself the revision of an earlier statement" (no. 2).

3   The Supplemental Move

The Background

One of the advantages of the widespread distribution and generally positive reception of *Music in Catholic Worship* (MCW) in the United States, and even in some other English-speaking countries, was that it was studied in classrooms[1] and widely discussed at national and regional meetings. More than that, however, it was one of those rare episcopal documents that was assiduously read by countless parish liturgy teams in their search for accessible guidelines and commonsense directions for the planning of local worship and the training of parochial musicians. On the other hand, the downside of such exposure to and consumption of this document was that the range of opinions about its theology and structure, guidelines and ritual analysis, and especially the three judgments, was magnified exponentially. Unlike almost any other previous liturgical directive from the US bishops, this teaching seems to have evoked an opinion from everyone, from celebrated organists and choir directors to professors of liturgy and diocesan directors of offices of worship to amateur guitarists and volunteer choir members.

In some ways MCW authorized and warranted this democracy of opinions by the very design of the three "decisions" at the heart of the document, borrowed from *The Place of Music in Eucharistic Celebrations* (PMEC). Professional musicians rightly believed that they had something important to say about the musical judgment, just as those who coordinated liturgies at national, diocesan, or local levels believed that

1. I employed the document in both my undergraduate and graduate teaching in the late 1970s, in imitation of others who had done so before me.

they had something valuable to say about the liturgical judgment. And then there were the ordinary folk in the pew, often represented on those many parish liturgy committees that thrived in the 1970s and 1980s, who certainly believed they had something to say not only about the pastoral judgment but about the other two as well.

To Correct or Not to Correct?

Almost from the beginning there was some energy to amend, correct, or replace MCW with a third-generation document. Father Patrick Collins, for example, remembers that very soon after its publication there were strong objections to paragraph 6's bald statement: "Good celebrations foster and nourish faith. Poor celebrations weaken and destroy faith."[2] At the same time, because of the wide acceptance of the document and its pastoral impact at so many levels, there was great resistance to any reediting of the document for fear that some of its most valuable contributions would be compromised. This was a topic of consideration at the annual gatherings of the FDLC, both in informal conversation and on the open floor of the plenary sessions of those gatherings. One of the collaborators on the original document, for example, has a vivid memory of Fr. Eugene Walsh taking the floor at one of those meetings and warning what could be lost if the document was revised too soon.

Another challenge to the document was the burgeoning of liturgical scholarship in the country that gave birth to MCW. When it was originally approved there was not a single university in the United States that had yet granted a PhD in liturgical studies.[3] By the turn of the decade, however, a school like Notre Dame not only had conferred a number of such doctorates but had established a department anchored by five significant figures in the field[4] and had almost 20 PhD students or candidates on its roster,[5] not to mention over 150 Master's

---

2. In the 1983 "corrected" version of MCW that statement was changed to the equally unsatisfying "Good celebrations foster and nourish faith. Poor celebrations may weaken and destroy it." This would be corrected in STTL, as discussed in the following chapter.

3. See above, chap. 2, n. 12.

4. Edward Kilmartin, Niels Rasmussen, Mark Searle, William Storey, and Robert Taft.

5. These included the likes of Andrew Ciferni, Kathleen Hughes, and Nathan Mitchell.

students in its celebrated summer program. These thriving programs generated volumes of research and, probably more importantly, serious reflection on liturgical principles, history, and methods that implicitly challenged some elements in MCW.

For example, one of the strengths of MCW—and its predecessor—was the help it provided for parsing primary from secondary or tertiary elements of the liturgy. By doing so it helped musicians prioritize the elements to be sung and suggested a type of planning that could be characterized as "planning from the inside out" (i.e., from primary to secondary elements) rather than a chronological pattern that simply began with the opening song and moved sequentially through the eucharistic rite. It prioritized the musical elements by grouping them in the following categories and order: (1) Acclamations (nos. 53–59), (2) Processional Songs (nos. 60–62), (3) Responsorial Psalms (no. 63), (4) Ordinary Chants (nos. 64–69), and (5) Supplemental Songs (nos. 70–74).

This somewhat rudimentary framework, however, often led to questionable conclusions. For example, MCW posits the five acclamations[6] as primary, not only by considering them first in this sequence but also by directing that they "ought to be sung even at Masses in which little else is sung." This principle suggests that the doxology to the Lord's Prayer has musical priority over the processional song at communion and even the responsorial psalm, an interpretation that is resoundingly rejected today. Furthermore, the "Lamb of God," which accompanies one of the most significant actions of the eucharistic liturgy (the fraction rite), is categorized among the "ordinary chants," which suggests that the doxology to the Lord's Prayer should receive more musical prominence than this central litany.

The increased scrutiny MCW received in the burgeoning liturgical programs around the United States began to reveal these and other problems with some aspects of its conception and design. Furthermore, the 1970s witnessed the appearance in rapid succession of many revised rites with major musical implications. These first appeared in an official Latin form (*editio typica* or "typical edition"), then in provisional translations (the so-called Green Book[7] from ICEL), and then

---

6. I.e., the Alleluia; Holy, Holy, Holy; Memorial Acclamation; Great Amen; and the doxology to the Lord's Prayer.

7. When these various translations were sent to the bishops, they were literally in green, and subsequently in white covers to distinguish provisional from final translations of the Latin text.

in the final English translations from ICEL (the so-called White Book).[8]
These included:

> The Liturgy of the Hours
>> editio typica: 1971; Green Book: 1974; White Book: 1974[9]
> The Rite of Christian Initiation of Adults
>> editio typica: 1972; Green Book: 1974; White Book of the General
>> Introduction: 1983; White Book of the ritual: 1986
> The Rite of Marriage
>> editio typica: 1969; Green Book: 1969; White Book: 1969
> The Rite of Funerals
>> provisional Green Book: 1967; editio typica: 1969; White Book: 1970.

The appearance of these liturgies in English (even in a provisional
state), and often their celebration in the vernacular even before official
vernacular translations were available, revealed MCW's relative weak-
ness in addressing the role of music in liturgical celebrations besides
the Eucharist. Pastors, liturgists, and musicians were clamoring for
some direction with these new rites. The Bishops' Committee on the
Liturgy (BCL) was under serious pressure, from many quarters, to
provide a somewhat comprehensive and coherent response.

A Prophetic Decision

Predicting the future is always dangerous. While the liturgical
leadership of the BCL in 1982 may not have understood the ramifica-
tions of their decision, as we will see in the next chapter, these decisions
were significant, especially in the move to affirm continuity over dis-
continuity. The choice, in a word, was to "supplement" rather than
"replace." Whether the underlying motivation was reading the signs
of the times or concern about losing what had already been gained,
whether it was a commitment to open new ground or hold on to hard-
fought territory, the decision in 1982 was clear: MCW would not be
rewritten. Instead, a supplementary document would be commissioned,
drafted, reworked, and issued. It would also be explicit in celebrating

---

8. I am grateful to my colleague Gilbert Ostdiek, OFM—longtime member and
former vice-chair of ICEL—for his firsthand documentation and chronology of this
process.

9. There were a host of interim English translations available as early as 1971, including the FDLC-sponsored Prayer of Christians: American Interim Breviary (New York:
Catholic Book Publishing, 1971).

its predecessor (MCW) while only footnoting the aboriginal role of PMEC.[10]

Unlike the previous documents from the BCL, *Liturgical Music Today* (LMT) was not the work of a committee. Rather, members of the secretariat of the BCL apparently approached three individuals to write various drafts of the proposed document. The author of the draft that was finally accepted reports that he saw neither of the previous drafts, was given little instruction for the writing process, and was simply told "you know what we want."[11] As this individual had been part of the FDLC and attended the meetings in which possible revisions of MCW had been discussed, he was well informed about the various debates surrounding MCW and the concern to produce something new without losing what had already been accomplished. He reports that a first draft was prepared and circulated to advisors and the comments returned to him. In reflecting on the comments, he noted: "It was a case of no one knowing exactly what they wanted, but they most certainly knew what they did not want." That included, for example, an assertion in the original draft that the standard of unaccompanied vocal chant (especially during Lent) could not be maintained, as well as a suggestion in that draft that instrumental accompaniment of presiders' chants should be possible in some contexts, for example, in African-American communities.

The outline of LMT demonstrates the supplemental nature of this document, which is approximately five hundred words shorter than its predecessor:

> Introduction (1–5)
> General Principles (6–14)
> > The Structure of the Liturgy (6–7)
> > The Place of Song (8)
> > The Function of Song (9–10)
> > The Form of Song (11)
> > Pastoral Concerns (12)

10. *Liturgical Music Today* (LMT), n. 1.

11. Personal e-mail from author, 29 March 2008; subsequently I interviewed the author by telephone on 14 April 2008. Both of these are my primary sources for reconstructing this process and relating the author's insights, although there has been collaboration on many points by others (e.g., some who served on the BCL secretariat at the time as well as another individual who submitted a draft of this document that was ultimately rejected).

As we work our way through the outline we see that the first clue to LMT's supplementary nature is its introduction, which is more historical than the theological introduction found in MCW and PMEC. Furthermore, the introduction itself notes that LMT should be read as a companion to MCW as well as to the 1978 statement from the BCL, *Environment and Art in Catholic Worship* (EACW, no. 3). Next, LMT enunciates a set of general principles (nos. 6–14) that do not find a parallel in MCW but seem to point to questions and issues that had arisen since the publication of MCW. The supplementary nature of

LMT is also highlighted in the fact that specific treatment of the eucharistic liturgy is virtually its briefest section, while it received the most attention in MCW. Conversely, LMT dedicates a proportionately larger section to a consideration of the sacraments, and a decidedly larger portion to musical reflections on the Liturgy of the Hours, which receive only two fleeting mentions in MCW (nos. 24 and 44). Most telling is that well over a third of the document addresses a conglomerate of issues gathered under the heading of "Other Matters." This, more than any other segment of LMT, symbolizes not only the fact that MCW did not address some key issues but even more that many new concerns had arisen since MCW was approved regarding topics that were hardly on the horizon in 1972.

The Contributions

Functionalism: When asked about what he considered the main contributions of LMT, the author of the finally accepted draft immediately underscored two major elements he considered central. First was the "treatment of how music functions sometimes as a rite itself, though more often as an accompaniment to a rite." The emphasis on "function"— or its correlative principle, often articulated as "functionalism"—was not born of liturgical or even musical thinking. For example, in his celebrated *The Rules of Sociological Method*, Émile Durkheim (d. 1917) notes that "the physiologist studies the functions of the average organism; the same is true of the sociologist,"[12] evidence for why Durkheim is often considered the founder of the functional sociological paradigm. About the same time there was a movement in architecture closely associated with the Chicago architect Louis Sullivan (d. 1924), whose famous maxim was "form ever follows function."[13] The movement itself was thus known as functionalism. Eventually in music, prominent figures in the new field of "anthropology of music" such as Alan Merriam were writing in the early 1960s about the various "functions"

12. Émile Durkheim, *The Rules of Sociological Method and Selected Texts on Sociology and its Method*, ed. with introduction by Steven Lukes, trans. W. D. Halls (London: Macmillan, 1982), 92.
13. Louis H. Sullivan, "The tall office building artistically considered," *Lippincott's Magazine* 57 (March 1896): 403–9, online at http://ocw.mit.edu/OcwWeb/Civil-and-Environmental-Engineering/1-012Spring2002/Readings/detail/-The-Tall-Office-Building-Artistically-Considered-.htm (accessed 4 December 2008).

of music in a society, and how that was defining a new field of study eventually known as ethnomusicology.[14]

The liturgical foundation for this "functional" move is found in the *Constitution on the Sacred Liturgy*. In 1903, Pope Pius X had argued that music must be holy and "exclude all profanity not only in itself but also in the manner in which it is presented."[15] Although this norm recognizes the possibility of a profane performance, it also admits that music, apart from any usage, has the potential for profanity in and of itself. From this viewpoint the most appropriate music for worship was thought to be music that possessed "in the highest degree the qualities proper to the liturgy . . . precisely sanctity"[16] or holiness. Thus "sacred music" was not first of all a name designating some sacred usage, but music that in itself possessed the attribute of sanctity. Pius X goes on to assert that the supreme model for sacred music has always been Gregorian Chant, and music is evaluated according to how closely it conforms to this model. Thus he concludes: "the more out of harmony 'any composition' is with that supreme model, the less worthy it is of the temple."[17]

A significant departure from this approach, already foreshadowed in the 1955 encyclical of Pope Pius XII (d. 1958), *Musicae sacrae disciplina*,[18] was made explicit in the Constitution on the Sacred Liturgy, which did not rely heavily on abstract philosophical or theological criteria for evaluating worship music but precisely emphasized the *function* of sacred music. Thus CSL notes that it is in the wedding of music to words that music "forms a necessary or integral part of the solemn liturgy" (no. 112). Even more significant in this regard is the

14. See, for example, his *The Anthropology of Music* (Evanston, IL: Northwestern University Press, 1964), 209–29, in which he outlines ten clear functions of music in societies.

15. *Tra le Sollecitudini* 2, as cited in R. Kevin Seasoltz, *The New Liturgy: A Documentation, 1903–1965* (New York: Herder and Herder, 1966), 5.

16. Ibid.

17. *Tra le Sollecitudini* 3, in Seasoltz, *The New Liturgy*, 5.

18. See, for example, the discussion beginning at paragraph 30 on the role of sacred music in the "actual performance" of the rites, music's power "to embellish the voices of the priest . . . and of the Christian people" (31), its ability to make the community's prayer more effective (31), and its power to "increase the honor given to God . . . [and] increase the fruits which the faithful . . . derive from the holy Liturgy" (32). Finally, the encyclical actually notes that nothing can be "more exalted or sublime than its *function* of accompanying . . . the voice of the priest . . . with the people" (34), and adds to "this highest function" another, i.e., "accompanying and beautifying other liturgical ceremonies." Ibid., 223–24.

statement that "sacred music is to be considered the more holy, the more closely connected it is with the liturgical action, whether making prayer more pleasing, promoting unity of minds, or conferring greater solemnity on the sacred rites" (no. 112). While employing language of holiness reminiscent of Pius X, CSL clearly moved toward what could be a more functional definition of sacred music, stressing that its holiness is not only or essentially a matter of ontology or ethics but, instead, is related to music's ability to wed itself to text and rite.

It is this turn toward a more functional understanding of liturgical music that occupies LMT throughout most of the general principles and is especially explicated in numbers 9 and 10 on "The Function of Song." In these brief introductory paragraphs, while building on the insights of its predecessor documents, LMT helps us to understanding that liturgical music is not only "in" the ritual or accompaniment to ritual action, but sometimes the music is the "constituent element of the rite." Thus while MCW had helped us understand that we were to sing some Mass parts rather than others because of their intrinsic liturgical value or importance, LMT goes further and prods liturgists and musicians alike to determine how a particular piece of liturgical music was actually functioning within the rite. Such analysis had the potential to contribute to effectiveness in choosing and performing such music in view of its given function(s).[19]

Psalms: The author's sense of the second major contribution of LMT was the attention given to the Liturgy of the Hours in general and to psalmody in particular. As noted above, the official English translation of the Liturgy of the Hours became available in 1974, and by 1976 major publishers had made the entire four-volume translation available in the United States. Previous to that, however, there were not only a number of interim English breviaries published for clergy and religious[20] but also a growing number of sophisticated resources for the celebration of morning and evening prayer by the laity.[21] The

19. Between CSL and LMT this functional aspect of music had been explored by Bernard Huijbers, among others. See, for example, his *The Performing Audience: Six and a Half Essays on Music and Song in Liturgy*, 2nd ed. (Cincinnati: North American Liturgy Resources, 1974).

20. See n. 9 above.

21. One of the most enduring of these was *Morning Praise and Evensong*, ed. William Storey and others (Notre Dame, IN: Fides Publishers, 1973), which reappeared six years later as *Praise God in Song*, ed. John Melloh and William Storey (Chicago: GIA Publications, 1979).

growing interest in both study and celebration of the Liturgy of the Hours had already prompted the Bishops' Committee on the Liturgy to issue one of the "study texts" on the Liturgy of the Hours.[22] While relatively good on the theology and structure of the rites, that study text was less good about music in the Liturgy of the Hours and especially the various methods for singing the psalms, which get the majority of the attention in this section of LMT.[23]

The value of this section is not only in the specifics about psalm singing but also in the underlying message about the inherent musicality of the psalms and the importance of singing them not only in the Liturgy of the Hours but in the Eucharist, other sacramental celebrations, and wherever they are employed. Roman Catholics had been used to singing hymns at worship, and occasionally part of the Ordinary of the Mass, but psalms were not an ordinary part of their liturgical repertoire in the United States. Thus this section of LMT was a valuable impetus to that growing trend in Roman Catholic worship.

Signaling the future: As noted above, the longest section of LMT is a conglomerate of issues and ideas gathered under the banner of "Other Matters." Most of the seven issues treated there will continue to occupy liturgical musicians, liturgists, and church leaders for decades to come and are themes that will return in *Sing to the Lord*. For example, this is one of the first music documents that gives explicit consideration to issues of music and culture. LMT appeared the same year that Anscar Chupungco published his groundbreaking *Cultural Adaptation of the Liturgy*,[24] before which there was precious little of any quality written on the subject in English. Since then there has been an avalanche of writing on this topic in English, as well as the 1994 fourth instruction, "For the Right Implementation of the Constitution on the Sacred Liturgy of the Second Vatican Council," which appears as *Inculturation and the Roman Liturgy* (*Varietates Legitimae*).

LMT gives the most attention in this section to "music ministry." While MCW did provide a paragraph (no. 77) stressing the need for "qualified musicians" and the church's responsibility to provide just compensation for them, and spent some time outlining various musical

22. *Study Text VII: The Liturgy of the Hours* (Washington, DC: USCC, 1981).

23. There is one problem in this section, i.e., a historically inaccurate definition of "antiphonal." The corrective is found in Robert Taft, "The Structural Analysis of Liturgical Units: An Essay in Methodology," *Worship* 52, no. 4 (1978): 321–29.

24. Anscar Chupungco, *Cultural Adaptation of the Liturgy* (New York: Paulist Press, 1982).

roles (nos. 35–38), that document offered very little theological reflection on the nature of this service. One important context for the eight paragraphs (nos. 63–70) on music ministry in LMT was undoubtedly the founding of the National Association of Pastoral Musicians in 1976, whose first national meeting in 1978 drew over 1700 participants and by the early 1980s had nearly five thousand members. LMT is actually the first bishops' document to speak about "pastoral musicians" (no. 63) and use that generic term for referencing all the musical specialists who lead assemblies in worship. While reiterating some of MCW's emphases on quality, training, and compensation, LMT is more intentional about providing something of a theological foundation for this ministry defined in terms of discipleship and not simply musicianship.

Finally, LMT for the first time broaches the issue of recorded music within worship (nos. 60–62). While this was a brave beginning, since the document was written in the midst of a technological revolution in the music industry there were many things it could not foresee. Cassette recordings were introduced in the 1960s, and by the 1980s their sales passed those of LP records. Dolby and digital recording changed the industry in the 1970s, and the compact disk became commercially available in 1983, right after the publication of LMT. That was also the year that Yamaha introduced the first truly digital keyboard at an affordable price. While the principle in LMT that recorded music should "never be used within the liturgy to replace the congregation, the choir, the organist or other instrumentalists" pointed in the right direction, it was soon going to prove inadequate. This was true in terms of changing technology as well as the growing awareness of the needs of many rural communities who often could not find, hire, or offer the financial resources necessary to sustain even a part-time qualified musician.

Summary

In some ways LMT was as important for what it did *not* do as for what it did. What it did not do was replace MCW; instead, it offered itself as an intentional companion and supplement to MCW. By doing so it implicitly confirmed central contributions of MCW and extended the life of that document into the twenty-first century. While this may seem like an exaggeration to some, it appears to be documentable by the BCL itself. As we will explore more fully in the next chapter, when the BCL convened a public consultation in 2006 for the drafting of a new document, that consultation was entitled "A Consultation on a Revision of *Music in Catholic Worship.*" Furthermore, the official introduction to that consultation, penned by the then executive director of the bishops' secretariat for the liturgy, did not even refer to LMT, although it was mentioned by participants in the course of that consultation.

At the same time, LMT made its own contributions to the dialogue in the United States about liturgical music. It drew attention to sacraments and the Liturgy of the Hours, pointed to more nuanced understandings of the function of liturgical music, emphasized the intrinsically lyrical nature of psalmody, and furthered the dialogue about not only the role but also the vocation of the pastoral musician. In many respects its enduring contributions will be revisited in the next chapter when we illustrate just how many of the ideas in LMT, and even how much of its language, were incorporated into *Sing to the Lord.*

4 *Sing to the Lord*

The Background

A Shifting Climate

Many welcomed the decision not to rewrite *Music in Catholic Worship* (MCW) but to supplement it with a new and complimentary document, as outlined in the previous chapter. In the changing liturgical climate of the following decade it also came to be recognized as a highly unusual and maybe even prophetic move. *Liturgical Music Today* (LMT), however, was not without its critics, and the fact that it did not replace MCW with a document more accepting of the use of Latin, Gregorian Chant, and other traditional music was a source of concern to some. This concern grew during the 1980s as the Tridentine Mass received renewed attention and even support from the Vatican.

As early as 1980, Pope John Paul II had asked the bishops of the world to provide feedback about the reception of the Missal of 1970 and the liturgical reforms, and any resistance to those reforms. In response, despite the fact that the vast majority of the bishops of the world did not think there was a great clamoring for the Tridentine Rite, the Congregation for Divine Worship issued the circular letter *Quattuor Abhinc Annos* ("Four Years Later"), which "grants to diocesan bishops the possibility of using an indult whereby priests and faithful, who shall be expressly indicated in the letter of request to be presented to their own bishop, may be able to celebrate Mass by using the Roman Missal according to the 1962 edition."[1] Four years later the same pope

---

1. *Quattuor Abhinc Annos*, trans. in *L'Osservatore Romano*, English ed. (October 22, 1984), http://www.adoremus.org/Quattuorabhincannos.html (accessed December 10, 2008).

issued a *motu proprio* following the excommunication of Archbishop Marcel Lefebvre (d. 1991) and four bishops whom Lefebvre had consecrated to ensure the survival of his Priestly Fraternity of St. Pius X, which celebrated the Tridentine Rite. While condemning them in *Ecclesia Dei* ("God's Church"), the pope also wrote that "respect must everywhere be shown for the feelings of all those who are attached to the Latin liturgical tradition, by a wide and generous application of the directives already issued some time ago by the Apostolic See for the use of the Roman Missal according to the typical edition of 1962."[2]

This apparent shift in liturgical climate became more apparent in the 1990s with a series of what many considered high-profile liturgical "reversals" on the part of the Vatican vis-à-vis Roman Catholic worship in the United States. For example, in 1994 the Vatican withdrew its 1992 permission to employ the New Revised Standard Version of the Bible for liturgical use. Simultaneously, permission to use the Psalter from the Revised New American Bible for liturgical use, approved by the US bishops in 1991, was denied. The result was rejection of the lectionary the US bishops had submitted in 1992, which relied on these translations. In 1996 Rome required Bishop Anthony Pilla of Cleveland, then president of the NCCB, to withdraw the US bishops' imprimatur (given in 1995) from the Psalms translated by the International Commission on English in the Liturgy (ICEL). In 1997 Rome rejected the ordination rite the US bishops had approved and submitted in 1996 because of what Rome considered a flawed English translation.

Environment and Art in Catholic Worship Redux?

That the liturgical climate was shifting not only in Rome but also in the United States was clear from what many considered a comparable liturgical reversal regarding the 1978 document *Environment and Art in Catholic Worship* (EACW). As was customary at the time, and employing exactly the same procedure employed for MCW, EACW was not issued by the entire conference of bishops but by a committee of that conference. It was suggested that this provided the loophole

2. *Ecclesia Dei*, at http://www.vatican.va/holy_father/john_paul_ii/motu
_proprio/documents/hf_jp-ii_motu-proprio_02071988_ecclesia-dei_en.html (accessed December 10, 2008); in 2007 Pope Benedict XVI would extend this permission even further in his *Summorum Pontificum*, at http://www.vatican.va/holy_father/ benedict_xvi/motu_proprio/documents/hf_ben-xvi_motu-proprio_20070707 _summorum-pontificum_lt.html (accessed October 22, 2008).

for ignoring EACW, which was thought by some to be too secular a document.

As noted above in chapter two, however, in 1983, on the tenth anniversary of the promulgation of the CSL, the NCCB issued a pastoral statement entitled "The Church at Prayer," which states: ". . . our Committee on the Liturgy has issued statements which have been well received and proven very useful, especially *Music in Catholic Worship*, *Liturgical Music Today*, and *Environment and Art in Catholic Worship*. The norms and guidelines of these documents should be followed by pastors and all those engaged in the liturgical arts."[3] Nonetheless, criticism continued unabated, and many assailed EACW as too Protestant a document, one that ignores the church's tradition, is both architecturally and liturgically reductionistic,[4] inappropriately embraces modernistic principles of architecture, and "substitutes for a sacramental understanding of the church building a functionalist model whose job is to set a mood and provide for a hospitable environment."[5]

By the new millennium the US bishops were ready to issue a new document on liturgical environment that revealed a reversal in previous procedures, as it was not approved by any single committee of the USCCB but was voted on and approved by the entire conference at their November 2000 meeting. The introduction to *Built of Living Stones* (BLS) further makes it eminently clear that BLS was not a revision but a replacement of EACW. So the bishops write, "the bishops of the United States present a new document on church art and architecture that builds on and replaces *Environment and Art* and addresses the needs of the next generation of parishes engaged in building or renovating churches."

Some find BLS a welcome corrective to EACW, offering a more balanced vision of architecture and liturgical reform. Others question some of its theological presuppositions and wonder aloud whether it will have the broad and positive influence of its predecessor among both Roman Catholics and Protestants. Noted liturgical consultant

3. See above, chap. 2, n. 26.

4. Duncan Stroik, "Environment and Art in Catholic Worship—A Critique," *Sacred Architectural Journal*, http://www.sacredarchitecture.org/articles/ environment_and _art_in_catholic_worship_a_critique/ (accessed 11 December, 2008).

5. Denis McNamara, "Can We Keep Our Churches Catholic? A Critical Look at 'Environment and Art in Catholic Worship'—With Hope for the Future," *Adoremus Bulletin* 4, no. 4 (February–March 1998), http://www.adoremus.org/98-03_mcnamara .htm (accessed 11 December, 2008).

and art historian Marchita Mauck, for example, has written that BLS is preoccupied with the location and symbolism of the presider's chair, the separation of the sanctuary from the assembly, and is excessively concerned about the location of the tabernacle.[6]

In the wake of this apparent rejection by the US bishops of the approach and many central ideas of EACW, there was widespread anxiety that any document replacing MCW would result in similar reversals, undercutting many of its pivotal insights. Happily, those anxieties were not realized. Two factors seemed to enable this happy outcome. One was that, under the leadership of Bishop Edward Grosz, the music subcommittee[7] of the BCL actually held a public hearing in October 2006 as part of the process toward crafting the new document. More than fifty representatives from across the musical-liturgical landscape provided input. After that public consultation the subcommittee continued to consult discreetly but relatively widely on a proposed draft of the new statement. A second factor appears to have been the deep respect the subcommittee and many consultors had for both MCW and LMT. As a result, *Sing to the Lord: Music in Divine Worship* (STTL) appears to be anything but a change in direction and truly emerges as an organic development from its predecessors. At the very beginning of STTL the bishops themselves acknowledge that this "is a revision of *Music in Catholic Worship*."

Sing to the Lord

The Structure and Design of STTL

STTL is comparatively long: three times the length of MCW and larger than the three previous documents combined. As demonstrated by its outline, this is the most comprehensive music document the US bishops have ever issued and, as we shall see, at the heart of the document are large sections from both MCW and LMT.

---

6. Marchita Mauck, "Architectural Setting (Modern)," *The New Westminster Dictionary of Liturgy and Worship*, ed. Paul Bradshaw (Louisville and London: Westminster John Knox, 2002), 25.

7. Members of the Subcommittee on Music in the Liturgy for the BCL were Bishop Edward Grosz (auxiliary, Buffalo), Bishop Patrick Cooney (Gaylord), Archbishop John G. Vlazny (Portland, Oregon), and Bishop Arthur J. Serratelli (Paterson). Advisors to the BCL Subcommittee on music were Robert Batastini; John Foley, SJ; J. Michael McMahon; Leo Nestor; and Anthony Ruff, OSB.

Reliance on MCW

The assertion by the bishops that STTL is a revision rather than a replacement of MCW is validated by multiple reliances of the new document on its predecessors. Sometimes that reliance is manifest in direct borrowing not only of ideas but even of key texts from MCW. For example, in its introductory section on "Why We Sing," STTL not only quotes MCW but also PMEC regarding the relationship between faith and liturgy:

STTL	MCW (1983)	PMEC
5. This common, sung expression of faith within liturgical celebrations strengthens our faith when it grows weak and draws us into the divinely inspired voice of the Church at prayer. Faith grows when it is well expressed in celebration. Good celebrations can foster and nourish faith. Poor celebrations may weaken it.	6. Faith grows when it is well expressed in celebration. Good celebrations foster and nourish faith. Poor celebrations may weaken and destroy it.	I. From this it is clear that the manner in which the Church celebrates the liturgy has an effect on the faith of men. Good celebrations foster and nourish faith. Poor celebrations weaken and destroy faith.

While reiterating MCW, STTL also introduces an important nuance paralleling that introduced into the 1983 version of MCW, now noting that "Good celebrations *can* foster and nourish faith." Similarly, STTL reiterates MCW's powerful insight about the role of the presider when it notes:

STTL	MCW (1983)
18. No other single factor affects the Liturgy as much as the attitude, style, and bearing of the priest celebrant, who "prays in the name of the Church and of the assembled community." "When he celebrates the Eucharist, . . . [the priest] must serve God and the people with dignity and humility, and by his bearing and by the way he says the divine words he must convey to the faithful the living presence of Christ."	21. No other single factor affects the liturgy as much as the attitude, style, and bearing of the celebrant: his sincere faith and warmth as he welcomes the worshipping community; his human naturalness combined with dignity and seriousness as he breaks the Bread of Word and Eucharist.

Again, while borrowing a strong insight as well as specific language, STTL also acknowledges shifts that have occurred since the writing of MCW and, for example, adopts the language of "priest celebrant" found in the 2003 *General Instruction of the Roman Missal,* adding a further quotation from that document (n. 32), supporting the use of this new language.

Probably the most identifiable citation from MCW and PMEC is STTL's embrace of a central contribution of those documents regarding the threefold judgment. Because this material is so celebrated and has undergone significant elaboration over the decades, it is worth citing at length:

STTL	*MCW* (1983)	*PMEC*
126. In judging the appropriateness of music for the Liturgy, one will examine its liturgical, pastoral, and musical qualities. Ultimately, however, these three judgments are but aspects of one evaluation, which answers the question: "Is this particular piece of music appropriate for this use in the particular Liturgy?" All three judgments must be considered together, and no individual judgment can be applied in isolation from the other two. This evaluation requires cooperation, consultation, collaboration, and mutual respect among those who are skilled in any of the three judgments, be they pastors, musicians, liturgists, or planners.	25. To determine the value of a given musical element in a liturgical celebration a threefold judgment must be made: musical, liturgical, and pastoral . . .	III. C. There are three judgments to be made about music in worship: musical, liturgical, pastoral. One of the major concerns of good celebrations is to select suitable music and perform it adequately. Such concern calls for different kinds of judgments . . .

STTL	MCW (1983)	PMEC
The Liturgical Judgment	The Liturgical Judgment	III. C. 2. The Liturgical Judgment
127. The question asked by this judgment may be stated as follows: Is this composition capable of meeting the structural and textual requirements set forth by the liturgical books for this particular rite?	32. Does the music express and interpret the text correctly and make it more meaningful? Is the form of the text respected?	The nature of the liturgy itself will help to determine what kind of music is called for, what parts are to be preferred for singing, and who is to sing them.
128. Structural considerations depend on the demands of the rite itself to guide the choice of parts to be sung, taking into account the principle of progressive solemnity (see nos. 110ff. in this document). A certain balance among the various elements of the Liturgy should be sought, so that less important elements do not overshadow more important ones. Textual elements include the ability of a musical setting to support the liturgical text and to convey meaning faithful to the teaching of the Church.	31. The choice of sung parts, the balance between them, and the style of musical setting used should reflect the relative importance of the parts of the Mass (or other service) and the nature of each part. Thus elaborate settings of the entrance song, "Lord have Mercy" and "Glory to God" may make the proclamation of the word seem unimportant; and an overly elaborate offertory song with a spoken "Holy, Holy, Holy Lord" may make the eucharistic prayer seem less important.	
129. A brief introduction to the aspects of music and the		

STTL	MCW (1983)	PMEC
various liturgical rites is provided below in nos. 137ff. Pastoral musicians should develop a working familiarity with the requirements of each rite through a study of the liturgical books themselves.		
The Pastoral Judgment	The Pastoral Judgment	III. C. 3. The Pastoral Judgment
130. The pastoral judgment takes into consideration the actual community gathered to celebrate in a particular place at a particular time. Does a musical composition promote the sanctification of the members of the liturgical assembly by drawing them closer to the holy mysteries being celebrated? Does it strengthen their formation in faith by opening their hearts to the mystery being celebrated on this occasion or in this season? Is it capable of expressing the faith that God has planted in their hearts and summoned them to celebrate?	39. The pastoral judgment governs the use and function of every element of celebration. Ideally this judgment is made by the planning team or committee. It is the judgment that must be made in this particular situation, in these concrete circumstances. Does music in the celebration enable these people to express their faith, in this place, in this age, in this culture?	The pastoral judgment must always be present. It is the judgment that must be made in this particular situation, in these concrete circumstances. Does music in the celebration enable these people to express their faith in this place, in this age, in this culture?

STTL	MCW (1983)	PMEC
131. In the dioceses of the United States of America today, liturgical assemblies are composed of people of many different nations. Such peoples often "have their own musical tradition, and this plays a great part in their religious and social life. For this reason their music should be held in proper esteem and a suitable place is to be given to it, not only in forming their religious sense but also in adapting worship to their native genius . . . ."		
132. Other factors—such as the age, culture, language, and education of a given liturgical assembly—must also be considered. Particular musical forms and the choice of individual compositions for congregational participation will often depend on those ways in which a particular group finds it easiest to join their hearts and minds to the liturgical action. Similarly, the musical	41. A musician may judge that a certain composition or style of composition is good music, but this musical judgment really says nothing about whether and how this music is to be used in this celebration. The signs of the celebration must be accepted and received as meaningful for a genuinely human faith experience for these specific worshipers. This pastoral judgment	A musician may say, for instance, that Gregorian Chant is good music. His musical judgment really says nothing about whether and how it is to be used in this celebration. The signs of the celebration must be accepted and received as meaningful. They must, by reason of the materials used, open up to a genuinely human faith experience. This pastoral judgment can be aided by sociological

STTL	MCW (1983)	PMEC
experience of a given liturgical assembly is to be carefully considered, lest forms of musical expression that are alien to their way of worshipping be introduced precipitously. On the other hand, one should never underestimate the ability of persons of all ages, cultures, languages, and levels of education to learn something new and to understand things that are properly and thoroughly introduced.	can be aided by sensitivity to the cultural and social characteristics of the people who make up the congregation: their age, culture, and education.	studies of the people who make up the congregation, studies which determine differences in age, culture, and education, as they influence the way in which faith is meaning fully expressed. No set of rubrics or regulations of itself will ever achieve a truly pastoral celebration of the sacramental rites. Such regulations must always be applied with a pastoral concern for the given worshipping community.
133. The pastoral question, finally, is always the same: Will this composition draw this particular people closer to the mystery of Christ, which is at the heart of this liturgical celebration?		
The Musical Judgment	The Musical Judgment	III. C. 1. The Musical Judgment
134. The musical judgment asks whether this composition has the necessary aesthetic qualities that can bear the weight of the mysteries celebrated in theLiturgy. It asks the question: Is this composition	26. Is the music technically, aesthetically, and expressively good?	Is the music technically and aesthetically good?

STTL	MCW (1983)	PMEC
technically, aesthetically, and expressively worthy?		
135. This judgment requires musical competence. Only artistically sound music will be effective and endure over time. To admit to the Liturgy the cheap, the trite, or the musical cliché often found in secular popular songs is to cheapen the Liturgy, to expose it to ridicule, and to invite failure.	[26] This judgment is basic and primary and should be made by competent musicians. Only artistically sound music will be effective in the long run. To admit the cheap, the trite, the musical cliché often found in popular songs for the purpose of "instant liturgy" is to cheapen the liturgy, to expose it to ridicule, and to invite failure.	This question should be answered by competent musicians. This judgment is basic and primary.
136. Sufficiency of artistic expression, however, is not the same as musical style, for "the Church has not adopted any particular style of art as her own. She has admitted styles from every period, in keeping with the natural characteristics and conditions of peoples and the needs of the various rites." Thus, in recent times, the Church has consistently recognized and freely welcomed the use of various styles	28. We do a disservice to musical values, however, when we confuse the judgment of music with the judgment of musical style. Style and value are two distinct judgments. Good music of new styles is finding a happy home in the celebrations of today. To chant and polyphony we have effectively added the chorale hymn, restored responsorial singing to some extent, and employed many styles of	

STTL	MCW (1983)	PMEC
of music as an aid to liturgical worship.	contemporary compo-sition. Music in folk idiom is finding ac-ceptance in eucha-ristic celebrations. We must judge value within each style.	

While STTL is highly reliant on its predecessors for this section, it also demonstrates original thinking and introduces many useful nuances. First is the welcome explication STTL makes at the opening of the section that the three judgments are but aspects of one evaluation (no. 26). In doing so, STTL maintains the "judgment" language of MCW and PMEC but weaves them together in more of a seamless garment with the stress on a single evaluation.[8] Besides the many other changes and useful elaborations in this section, the most obvious and welcome is the fact that STTL has changed the original order of the judgments. While this could suggest that the leading issue one needs to consider when addressing liturgical music is the liturgical one, it more importantly seems to realign the musical judgment and move it from the privileged place it occupied in previous documents.

Reliance on LMT

What may be more surprising to readers of STTL is that, while the bishops have called it a "revision of *Music in Catholic Worship*," in many places STTL is equally reliant on sections of LMT. For example,

---

8. This direction was already signaled in the 1982 publication *The Milwaukee Symposia for Church Composers: A Ten-Year Report* (Chicago: Liturgy Training Publications, 1992), which critiqued MCW in this way: "One difficulty is the tendency to treat the musical-liturgical-pastoral judgment as three separate judgments. . . . MCW introduces the sections on this topic by noting that 'a threefold judgment must be made: musical, liturgical and pastoral.' Yet the ensuing sections of MCW contribute to a fragmentation of this single, multifaceted judgment by treating the musical, liturgical and pastoral aspects separately, without any discussion of their integration. . . . Thus the various judgments—especially the musical and the pastoral—are sometimes perceived to be in opposition to each other. To avoid such conflicts and to respect more completely the formulation found in MCW, it is necessary to admit of a single, multifaceted judgment for evaluating musical elements in worship" (no. 82).

while STTL has a more extended discussion of the psalmist and cantor, it clearly builds on LMT's insights here.

STTL	LMT
34. The psalmist, or "cantor of the psalm," proclaims the Psalm after the first reading and leads the gathered assembly in singing the refrain. The psalmist may also, when necessary, intone the Gospel Acclamation and verse. Although this ministry is distinct from the role of the cantor, the two ministries are often entrusted to the same person.	69. The cantor's role is distinct from that of the psalmist, whose ministry is the singing of the verses of the responsorial psalm and communion psalm. Frequently the two roles will be combined in one person.
38. As a leader of congregational song, the cantor should take part in singing with the entire gathered assembly. In order to promote the singing of the liturgical assembly, the cantor's voice should not be heard above the congregation. As a transitional practice, the voice of the cantor might need to be amplified to stimulate and lead congregational singing when this is still weak. However, as the congregation finds its voice and sings with increasing confidence, the cantor's voice should correspondingly recede. At times, it may be appropriate to use a modest gesture that invites participation and clearly indicates when the congregation is to begin, but gestures should be used sparingly and only when genuinely needed.	68. Among music ministers, the cantor has come to be recognized as having a crucial role in the development of congregational singing. Besides being qualified to lead singing, he or she must have the skills to introduce and teach new music, and to encourage the assembly. This must be done with sensitivity so that the cantor does not intrude on the communal prayer or become manipulative. Introductions and announcements should be brief and avoid a homiletic style.

A similar relationship between STTL and LMT can be seen in the discussion of instrumental music (nos. 41–43 in the former and nos. 56–59 in the latter). An even more direct borrowing is obvious in the discussion of musicians as ministers.

STTL	LMT
48. The whole assembly is actively involved in the music of the Liturgy. Some members of the community, however, are recognized for the special gifts they exhibit in leading the musical praise and thanksgiving of Christian assemblies. These are the liturgical musicians, as described in section E, above, and their ministry is especially cherished by the Church.	63. The entire worshipping assembly exercises a ministry of music. Some members of the community, however, are recognized for the special gifts they exhibit in leading the musical praise and thanksgiving of Christian assemblies. These are the pastoral musicians, whose ministry is especially cherished by the Church.
49. Liturgical musicians are first of all disciples, and only then are they ministers. Joined to Christ through the Sacraments of Initiation, musicians belong to the assembly of the baptized faithful; they are worshipers above all else. Like other baptized members of the assembly, pastoral musicians need to hear the Gospel, experience conversion, profess faith in Christ, and so proclaim the praise of God. Thus, musicians who serve the Church at prayer are not merely employees or volunteers. They are ministers who share the faith, serve the community, and express the love of God and neighbor through music.	64. What motivates the pastoral musician? Why does he or she give so much time and effort to the service of the church at prayer? The only answer can be that the church musician is first a disciple and then a minister. The musician belongs first of all to the assembly; he or she is a worshipper above all. Like any member of the assembly, the pastoral musician needs to be a believer, needs to experience conversion, needs to hear the Gospel and so proclaim the praise of God. Thus, the pastoral musician is not merely an employee or volunteer. He or she is a minister, someone who shares faith, serves the community, and expresses the love of God and neighbor through music.

Another direct borrowing from LMT concerns the role of recorded music:

STTL	LMT
93. Recorded music lacks the authenticity provided by a living liturgical assembly gathered for the	60. Music, being preeminent among these things, ought to be "live." While recorded music,

STTL	LMT
Sacred Liturgy. While recorded music might be used advantageously outside the Liturgy as an aid in the teaching of new music, it should not, as a general norm, be used within the Liturgy.	therefore, might be used to advantage outside the liturgy as an aid in the teaching of new music, it should, as a norm, never be used within the liturgy to replace the congregation, the choir, the organist or other instrumentalists.
94. Some exceptions to this principle should be noted. Recorded music may be used to accompany the community's song during a procession outside and, when used carefully, in Masses with children. Occasionally, it might be used as an aid to prayer, for example, during long periods of silence in a communal celebration of reconciliation. However, recorded music should never become a substitute for the community's singing.	61. Some exceptions to this principle should be noted, however. Recorded music may be used to accompany the community's song during a procession out-of-doors and, when used carefully, in Masses with children. Occasionally it might be used as an aid to prayer, for example, during long periods of silence in a communal celebration of reconciliation. It may never become a substitute for the community's song, however, as in the case of the responsorial psalm after a reading from Scripture or during the optional hymn of praise after communion.

Besides such direct borrowing, STTL echoes important themes sounded in LMT, including cultural diversity (STTL nos. 57–60, LMT nos. 54–55), copyright issues (STTL nos. 105–6, LMT no. 71), and especially the section on the Liturgy of the Hours (STTL nos. 230–40, LMT nos. 34–45).[9] This consistent borrowing of both themes and texts from LMT, many of which have no parallel in MCW, reveals that STTL is more than a revision of MCW; rather, it is a revision of both MCW *and* LMT.

9. This includes repeating the erroneous definition of "antiphonal" found in LMT; see chap. 3, n. 25 above.

STTL is not simply repetitive of old ideas, however, and like its predecessors offers real developments, fresh insights, and some quite splendid new formulations. Like MCW it opens with a theological reflection, this time on "why we sing." Its first nine paragraphs echo some previous insights of its predecessor documents but also weave together singing and the paschal mystery with a strong social justice overtone that echoes the opening lines of *Gaudium et Spes*. Its introduction to liturgical participation (no. 10) is inventively rooted in Trinitarian and communion theologies.

STTL fills important lacunae in its predecessors, for example, addressing the pivotal leadership role of local bishops and offices of worship (nos. 16–17), a statement most welcome in a time when many worship offices are closing and the once vibrant FDLC is a shadow of its former self. There is a very fine section on the "Gathered Liturgical Assembly" (nos. 24–27), with an especially smart paragraph on the holy people singing with "one voice" (no. 27). This section is balanced with another quite intelligent section on the choir (nos. 28–33), a topic some felt had been neglected in previous music documents. New is the rich reflection (no. 43) on instrumental improvisation, as well as attention to the role of liturgical music in Catholic schools (nos. 54–56). There is also an intelligent discussion of Latin in the liturgy (nos. 61–66), which makes excellent points concerning the vernacular as the norm (no. 61), the importance of singing with understanding (no. 63), and the recognition that when the language poses an obstacle to singers "it would be more prudent to employ a vernacular language in the Liturgy" (no. 64). There is a very reasonable section on Gregorian Chant in STTL (nos. 72–80); especially useful is no. 73, which is worth quoting in its entirety:

> 73. The "pride of place" given to Gregorian chant by the Second Vatican Council is modified by the important phrase "other things being equal." These "other things" are the important liturgical and pastoral concerns facing every bishop, pastor, and liturgical musician. In considering the use of the treasures of chant, pastors and liturgical musicians should take care that the congregation is able to participate in the Liturgy with song. They should be sensitive to the cultural and spiritual milieu of their communities in order to build up the Church in unity and peace.

This nuanced paragraph demonstrates STTL's ability to recognize various important musical strands in our tradition while continuing to emphasize the primacy of the congregation's song—something STTL does with consistency and conviction.[10]

STTL is not without its flaws, and sometimes the seams show in a document drafted by committee, as it appears there was no single or primary author of STTL; instead, its different sections were authored by various members of the BCL subcommittee on Liturgy and Music, members of the BCL secretariat,[11] or other consultants. For example, there seems to be an inconsistency in defining the "liturgical assembly," which in number 10 is described as including the bishop, priest, deacon, acolytes, ministers of the Word, music leaders, choir, extraordinary ministers of Holy Communion, and the congregation; also, in number 11, STTL clearly distinguishes between the "gathered assembly" and the particular role of the "congregation." On the other hand, the section on "the gathered liturgical assembly" (nos. 24–27) seems to refer only to the "congregation" and not to the other ministers.

In the spirit of the current age there are more corrective instructions than in previous documents, for example, that the Sign of Peace "must not be protracted by the singing of a song." There is also misplaced emphasis on singing the "dialogues" in the liturgy (e.g., no. 115a), repeating an emphasis found in the *General Instruction of the Roman Missal* (no. 40), which inappropriately relies on the 1967 document *Musicam Sacram*.[12] Probably the most serious gaffe in the originally approved form, published as a .pdf file on the Internet, was omitting the "offering" when listing the various elements in the Eucharistic Prayer (no. 177). When this was brought to the attention of the BCL secretariat they were able to correct that error before the work was published as a single fascicle by the USCC publishing house in the summer of 2008.

---

10. E.g., nos. 19, 21, 22, 28, 31, 38, 42, 72, 85, 101, 103, 104, 122, 257, etc.

11. At the time, the director of the BCL secretariat was Msgr. James Moroney and the assistant director was Msgr. Anthony Sherman.

12. If the logic of this argument was pushed to its limit one could suggest that singing the greeting before the opening prayer ("The Lord be with You") is of higher liturgical priority than singing the *Sanctus*. See my "*Musicam Sacram* Revisited: Anchor to the Past or Path to the Future," *Studia Canonica* 42, no. 1 (2008): 69.

Summary

STTL is a fine pastoral document on music *and* liturgy—and not simply about music *in* the liturgy—exhibiting unusual musical breadth and sustained liturgical-pastoral intelligence. This most comprehensive music document from the US bishops (and one of the most comprehensive issued by any conference of Roman Catholic bishops in the world) offers broad-ranging theological reflection and pastoral direction on a wide gamut of musical-liturgical issues. Recognizing some of the shifting tides in liturgical reform over the past decade, it broaches issues of the treasury of sacred music, Latin in the liturgy, and Gregorian Chant without ever compromising the underlying principle of the active participation of the people or the primacy of the assembly's song.

More than a laudable achievement, however, STTL stands as the most recent installation in an extraordinary group of musical-liturgical documents from the US bishops. Each, in its own way, makes both an individual and a cumulative contribution to musical liturgy in the Roman Catholic Church in the United States. Demonstrating few of the reversals seen in other documents, such as what we saw from EACW to BLS, STTL seems to confirm a fundamental trajectory of understanding and pastoral practice regarding musical liturgy in the United States. This understanding is marked by an informed acknowledgment and embrace of the ministerial role of music and liturgical musicians, in dialogue with a rich musical tradition and new visions of worship music, contextualized in one of the most multicultural countries in the world. STTL is not simply a fine Roman Catholic document but also a truly "catholic" one.

Finally, the process of public and private consultation surrounding the writing of this document needs to be held up as a true symbol of active participation in the liturgy of the church. Many voices and perspectives were invited into the shaping of STTL, and while there may not always be musical or liturgical agreement among those voices on every aspect of STTL, who could deny that the process of its formulation contributed to the *una voce dicentes* ("singing with one voice") that is the vision of Christian worship and the hope of Christian living.

Abbreviations

BCL   US Bishops' Committee on the Liturgy

CSL   Constitution on the Sacred Liturgy, 1963 document of the Second Vatican Council

EACW   *Environment and Art in Catholic Worship*, 1978 document of the US Bishops' Committee on the Liturgy

FDLC   Federation of Diocesan Liturgical Commissions

IO   *Inter Oecumenici*

LMT   *Liturgical Music Today*, 1982 document of the US Bishops' Committee on the Liturgy

MCW   *Music in Catholic Worship*, 1972 document of the US Bishops' Committee on the Liturgy, revised 1983

MS   *Musicam Sacram*

NCCB   National Conference of Catholic Bishops of the USA (until 1 July 2001)

NCWC   National Catholic Welfare Conference of the US bishops (1922–1966)

PMEC   *The Place of Music in Eucharistic Celebrations*, 1968 document of the US Bishops' Committee on the Liturgy

STTL   *Sing to the Lord: Music in Divine Worship*, 2007 document of the United States Conference of Catholic Bishops

USCC   United States Catholic Conference (until 1 July 2001)

USCCB   United States Conference of Catholic Bishops (since 1 July 2001)